T0154288

JOSH AZOUZ

Josh Azouz is an award-winning writer working across stage, screen and radio. Plays include *The Night After* (Headlong/ BBC Four), *The Mikvah Project* (Orange Tree Theatre, Yard Theatre and BBC Radio 4), *Buggy Baby* (Yard Theatre, Channel 4 Playwright Award), *Victoria's Knickers* (National Youth Theatre/Soho Theatre) and *10,000 Smarties* (Old Fire Station, Oxford).

Other Titles in this Series

Josh Azouz

ONCE UPON A TIME IN NAZI OCCUPIED TUNISIA

NICK HERN BOOKS

London

www.nickhernbooks.co.uk

A Nick Hern Book

Once Upon A Time in Nazi Occupied Tunisia first published in Great Britain in 2021 as a paperback original by Nick Hern Books Limited, The Glasshouse, 49a Goldhawk Road, London W12 8QP

Once Upon A Time in Nazi Occupied Tunisia copyright © 2021 Josh Azouz

Josh Azouz has asserted his moral right to be identified as the author of this work

Cover image: Émilie Chen

Designed and typeset by Nick Hern Books, London
Printed in the UK by Mimeo Ltd, Huntingdon, Cambridgeshire PE29 6XX

A CIP catalogue record for this book is available from the British Library

ISBN 978 1 83904 022 1

CAUTION   All rights whatsoever in this play are strictly reserved. Requests to reproduce the text in whole or in part should be addressed to the publisher.

Amateur Performing Rights   Applications for performance, including readings and excerpts, by amateurs in the English language throughout the world should be addressed to the Performing Rights Department, Nick Hern Books, The Glasshouse, 49a Goldhawk Road, London W12 8QP, *tel* +44 (0)20 8749 4953, *email* rights@nickhernbooks.co.uk, except as follows:

Australia: ORiGiN Theatrical, Level 1, 213 Clarence Street, Sydney NSW 2000, *tel* +61 (2) 8514 5201, *email* enquiries@originmusic.com.au, *web* www.origintheatrical.com.au

New Zealand: Play Bureau, PO Box 9013, St Clair, Dunedin 9047, *tel* (3) 455 9959, *email* info@playbureau.com

United States and Canada: United Agents, see below

Professional Performing Rights   Applications for performance by professionals in any medium and in any language throughout the world should be addressed to United Agents, 12–26 Lexington St, London W1F 0LE, *tel* +44 (0)20 3214 0800, *fax* +44 (0)20 3214 0801, *email* info@unitedagents.co.uk

No performance of any kind may be given unless a licence has been obtained. Applications should be made before rehearsals begin. Publication of this play does not necessarily indicate its availability for amateur performance.

Once Upon A Time in Nazi Occupied Tunisia was first performed at the Almeida Theatre, London, on 26 August 2021 (previews from 21 August), with the following cast:

GRANDMA	Adrian Edmondson
FAIZA	Laura Hanna
YOUSSEF	Ethan Kai
VICTOR	Pierro Niel-Mee
LOYS	Yasmin Paige
LITTLE FELLA	Daniel Rainford
Direction	Eleanor Rhode
Design	Max Johns
Light	Jess Bernberg
Sound	David Gregory
Casting	Ginny Schiller CDG
Assistant Director	Sepy Baghaei

ALMEIDA
THEATRE

The Almeida Theatre makes brave new work that asks big questions: of plays, of theatre and of the world around us.

Whether new work or reinvigorated classics, the Almeida brings together the most exciting artists to take risks; to provoke, inspire and surprise our audiences.

Recent highlights include Rupert Goold's productions of *Albion* (also broadcast on BBC Four) and his Olivier and Tony Award-winning production of *Ink* (also West End and Broadway); Rebecca Frecknall's Olivier Award-winning production of *Summer and Smoke* (also West End); and Robert Icke's productions of *Hamlet* (also West End and broadcast on BBC Two), *Mary Stuart* (also West End and UK tour) and *The Doctor* (due to transfer to the West End in 2022).

The Almeida Theatre is a registered charity and is dependent on the support of individuals, companies, trusts and foundations. The COVID-19 crisis has had a profound impact on our finances, halting most of our income from ticket sales and commercial activity. We need to raise more than £2m in the next 12 months to secure the future of the theatre, realise our artistic ambitions and connect with the widest possible audience. If you can support us at this time visit **almeida.co.uk/supportus**

Angel Coulby (Anna) and Wil Coban (James) in *Albion* by Mike Bartlett, directed by Rupert Goold at the Almeida Theatre (2020). Photo by Marc Brenner.

almeida.co.uk

Artistic Director **Rupert Goold**

Executive Director **Denise Wood**

Associate Director **Rebecca Frecknall**

🐦 @AlmeidaTheatre

📘 /almeidatheatre

📷 @almeida_theatre

Registered Charity no. 282167

Supported using public funding by
**ARTS COUNCIL
ENGLAND**

For Amanda

Acknowledgements

A special thank you to Eleanor Rhode and the original cast –
Adrian Edmondson, Laura Hanna, Ethan Kai, Pierro Niel-Mee,
Yasmin Paige, Daniel Rainford.

The writing process was informed by conversations and
readings from Khalid Abdalla, Chiraz Aich, Loys Azria,
Ebenezer Bamgboye, Stephanie Bain, Claire Belhassine, Cathy
Burkeman, Rabbi Israel Elia, Rupert Goold, Rida Hamidou,
Amy Hodge, Tara Jaffar, Ashley Scott Layton, Dr Daniel Lee,
Mourad Mazouz, Dr Haim Saadoun, Giles Smart & Ashleigh
Wheeler.

A final thank you to MUJU and the company that devised
Harissa.

Characters

LOYS, *female, mid-twenties*
YOUSSEF, *male, late twenties to thirties*
GRANDMA, *male, forties to fifties*
VICTOR, *male, late twenties*
FAIZA, *female, mid-twenties*
LITTLE FELLA, *male, late teens*

The languages spoken by these characters would have been French, Arabic, German and possibly Italian. Actors should perform in their own voice rather than affecting an accent.

Notes on the Text

... = an unspoken thought, a struggle to articulate a thought.

( ) = the word in brackets must be played by an actor, not voiced.

/ = indicates when the subsequent speaker should interrupt.

Extra spacing is an invitation for longer pauses, sustained periods of action.

This text went to press before the end of rehearsals and so may differ slightly from the play as performed.

1.1

MARCH 1943.
FOUR MONTHS INTO THE NAZI OCCUPATION OF
TUNISIA.
A LABOUR CAMP... 40KM FROM TUNIS.

A hot day.
Desolate, lush, craggy terrain.
VICTOR, *shaven-headed, is buried up to his neck in earth.*

Silence.

VICTOR *hums.*

YOUSSEF *enters.*

YOUSSEF. I've been sent.

Beat.

VICTOR. You've been sent...?

YOUSSEF. There's no easy way to say it.

VICTOR. Just say it.

YOUSSEF. Maybe I should just do it.

VICTOR. Do – do – what!?

YOUSSEF. God give me strength.

VICTOR. Oh no.

YOUSSEF. It's not what I want –

VICTOR. Oh god, please, no –

    VICTOR *furiously whispers the Shema prayer in Hebrew.*

YOUSSEF. I've been sent to urinate on your face.

VICTOR. Oh.

    Beat.

    Can you aim for my mouth?

YOUSSEF. That could be misinterpreted.

VICTOR. I'm thirsty.

YOUSSEF. Little Fella is watching.

VICTOR. Did Little Fella give the order?

YOUSSEF. Yes.

VICTOR. Shit.

YOUSSEF. Close your eyes.

VICTOR. I can't feel my throat – aim for the mouth!

YOUSSEF. He said urinate first, after give him a drink.

VICTOR. What are we waiting for then!?

YOUSSEF. It's… demeaning.

VICTOR. For whom?!

YOUSSEF. Both of us!

VICTOR. I'm burning alive out here!

YOUSSEF. It's been a morning!

VICTOR. Your folks must be so proud.

YOUSSEF. …when will you stop talking?

VICTOR. Soon, I'll be dead in a day.

YOUSSEF. The burial will be quick.

VICTOR. Why bother? Gundis will burrow through my face.

YOUSSEF. Calm down this isn't the pictures.

VICTOR. Spitzer came back with no eyes!

YOUSSEF. That wasn't gundis.

VICTOR. Then how'd he lose his eyes!?

YOUSSEF. Little Fella dug them out.

VICTOR. Oh god please just fucking piss on me already.

YOUSSEF *undoes his flies*.

Wine, beer, waterfalls

YOUSSEF. Shush.

VICTOR. Blood, milk, mint tea

YOUSSEF. Shut up!

VICTOR. The sea, the sea at midnight, the water glowing with
  phosphorous, crawl into the shallows, sink into the wet sand,
  and the little waves ripple over you, and the waves ripple, and
  the waves ripple, and the ripply waves ripple ripple – come
  on how many times do I need to say ripply fucking waves?!

YOUSSEF *does up his flies*.
VICTOR *starts barking like a dog*.
YOUSSEF *puts his hand over* VICTOR*'s mouth*.

YOUSSEF. You're going to get yourself killed.

VICTOR (*muffled*). I'm going mad!

YOUSSEF. Memento is watching –

VICTOR (*muffled*). Fuck Memento!

YOUSSEF. Be quiet!

VICTOR (*muffled*). Get off!

YOUSSEF. Promise you'll be quiet!

VICTOR (*muffled*). I promise.

YOUSSEF *removes his hand*.

Pause.

YOUSSEF. They'll go for a smoke soon.

VICTOR. I'd like a smoke.

YOUSSEF. After, someone will come to inspect.

VICTOR. What are they hoping to find?

YOUSSEF. God willing it's Grandma, he's the most reasonable.

VICTOR. Reasonable?! Grandma strapped Pinchas to a tank. Then he *sketched* him.

YOUSSEF. Can he draw?

VICTOR. In an impressionistic sort of way.

YOUSSEF. That's something, the others are without imagination.

VICTOR. We talking figurative painters or NAZIS!?

YOUSSEF. Be quiet!

VICTOR. Youssef Youssef Youssef!

YOUSSEF. What?!

VICTOR. When they finish with us, they'll turn on you.

YOUSSEF. That's not what it says on the uniform.

VICTOR. I'd laugh but my throat has turned to sand.

YOUSSEF (*pointing to his badge*). Free Arabia, in German and Arabic.

VICTOR. I can't take you seriously right now.

YOUSSEF. Shall I stone you?

VICTOR. Go on then. If Little Fella sees, he'll put in a good word, you'll get a bonus –

YOUSSEF. *Victor stop!*

VICTOR. You used to be a sweet boy, maybe not the sharpest tool, but a *sweet sweet* boy.

YOUSSEF *whips out a bottle with a straw.*

YOUSSEF. Quickly, they've gone for a smoke.

VICTOR *drinks.*

YOUSSEF *feeds* VICTOR *a piece of black bread.*

VICTOR. *Love* what they've done with the bread.

YOUSSEF. I'll pass your compliments on to the chef.

VICTOR *finishes.*

VICTOR. How's Faiza?

YOUSSEF. Fine.

VICTOR. Must have her hands full with Nazi callers.

YOUSSEF. They prefer Jewish girls so...

VICTOR. Faiza's a real beauty though. They start tapping Arabs – she'll be their first.

YOUSSEF. May your house burn down.

VICTOR. Bet you wish you were in bed with her now.

YOUSSEF. Stop it.

VICTOR. Are you big spoon or little spoon?

YOUSSEF....

VICTOR. To think. She could be spooning you right now.

YOUSSEF. Plenty of time for that in the future.

VICTOR. When?

YOUSSEF. When we lie in our beds as masters.

VICTOR. Where were those lines when you needed them?

YOUSSEF....I saw Loys last night.

VICTOR. ?

YOUSSEF. She had Faiza and I over for supper.

VICTOR. How is she?!

YOUSSEF. Well.

VICTOR. '*Well*', what does well mean?

YOUSSEF. She's, well – healthy.

VICTOR. Loys is healthy!?

YOUSSEF. What do you want me to say?!

VICTOR. Is she sleeping better?

YOUSSEF. Yes.

VICTOR. Any messages?

YOUSSEF. Says she's thinking about you all the time.

Beat.

VICTOR. She said the same thing two weeks ago.

YOUSSEF. What do you want from her, a poem?

VICTOR. There's no talk of rounding up the women?

YOUSSEF. No.

VICTOR. Youssef – tell me – is there!?

YOUSSEF. There isn't!

YOUSSEF *takes out a bottle of suncream and applies it to* VICTOR*'s face.*

VICTOR. You're like a djinn with the gifts.

YOUSSEF. Would you rather burn?

VICTOR. What did Loys make?

YOUSSEF. Cuttlefish.

VICTOR. Loys wouldn't eat that.

YOUSSEF. That's what Loys ate.

VICTOR. It's not kosher.

YOUSSEF. Next time I see her I'll tell her off.

VICTOR. It's out of character.

YOUSSEF. Why do you care what she ate?

VICTOR. I don't... I just...

What was she wearing?

YOUSSEF. A dress.

VICTOR. What type of dress?

YOUSSEF. ...the material floats.

VICTOR. Chiffon?

YOUSSEF. Is that what it's called?

VICTOR. Don't pretend you don't know.

YOUSSEF. I'm not pretending if you say chiffon, okay, a chiffon dress. And sapphire earrings.

VICTOR. Bit dressed up for a Tuesday.

YOUSSEF. Her and Faiza were trying things on.

YOUSSEF *applies a bit more cream.*

VICTOR. Did you talk about much?

YOUSSEF. ...the war... always the war...

VICTOR. What did you tell her about me?

YOUSSEF. What I always tell her.

VICTOR *smiles faintly.*

VICTOR *hums the song 'Mack the Knife'.*

YOUSSEF *unbuttons his flies and starts pissing on* VICTOR*'s face.*

VICTOR. What the fu–

YOUSSEF. Keep your mouth shut and eyes down.

> GRANDMA, *a Nazi officer, enters on a motorised sleigh driven by* LITTLE FELLA.

> YOUSSEF, *mid-piss, 'Sieg Heil's to* GRANDMA.

GRANDMA. Are the toilets out of service?

LITTLE FELLA. Nah, I've just dropped off the kids.

GRANDMA. Then I'm unaware of this native custom.

YOUSSEF. It was an order, Grandma.

GRANDMA. Was it now. From who?

> YOUSSEF *briefly glances at* LITTLE FELLA.

YOUSSEF. Memento.

GRANDMA. You report directly to Little Fella.

YOUSSEF. Apologies Grandma.

GRANDMA. What's it like?

YOUSSEF. Pardon?

GRANDMA. To urinate on a man's face.

YOUSSEF. I don't…
Um.
Alright.

GRANDMA. '*Alright*'?

YOUSSEF. I'm not good with words.

GRANDMA. Invent words, mix them up, start a sentence backwards. Listen to how I dance between German and French and Italian and you're keeping up. That's to be applauded. What's it like to urinate on a man's face?

YOUSSEF.…Liberating.

GRANDMA. Now there's a word.

On the way over here I see two vipers mating. Yes I know –
two vipers! They're tangled up, licking each other, it's
astonishing. Over a dune I spy another viper sidling its way
towards us. This third viper stops to watch the happy couple.
A minute passes. Another minute passes. The third viper
joins in! My eyes pop out of my skull. I look over at Little
Fella and he's completely unfazed. Three vipers making love
and he doesn't even break a sweat. Turns out Little Fella
used to work in a pet shop. (*To* LITTLE FELLA.) Tell them
what you told me.

LITTLE FELLA. Male snakes have two penises, females have
two vaginas.

GRANDMA. Making an orgy almost the default mode.

LITTLE FELLA. I'm not sure that's necessarily –

GRANDMA. Three vipers copulating – is it a sign?

YOUSSEF. What?

GRANDMA. Deploy your fine Tunisian mind Youssef, there
are no wrong answers, only invisible people.

YOUSSEF. Um.

GRANDMA. This is a chance for you to step out from under
his arsehole and think *independently*.

YOUSSEF....

GRANDMA. Speculate.

YOUSSEF. I don't know.

GRANDMA. Nobody knows but you have to put yourself out
there.

YOUSSEF. Nothing springs to mind.

GRANDMA. Be brave Youssef.

YOUSSEF. I'm sorry.

GRANDMA. Don't apologise.

YOUSSEF. What is it you want to hear?

GRANDMA. It's not about what I want to hear.

YOUSSEF. I'm sorry Grandma.

GRANDMA. Stop apologising.

YOUSSEF. Perhaps it means... it could mean... well two
snakes... another snake...
Grandma I'm (sorry)

GRANDMA. How are you going to lead if you don't learn to
fail?

YOUSSEF. With respect, I'm not sure I want to lead.

GRANDMA. Don't you want your own country?

YOUSSEF. With all the breath in my life.

GRANDMA. Then you're shirking responsibility.

YOUSSEF. With respect, there are many great Tunisians who
could lead. The Constitutionalists Party is full of them.

GRANDMA. That modesty makes you the perfect candidate.

YOUSSEF. I'm not your man. I'm terrible with a map, shy in
large groups – I have a lazy eye.

GRANDMA *sits on his sleigh.*
Stares at VICTOR.

GRANDMA. I was up all night thinking about you.

In Europe you'd be shot on the spot, but out here, we can be
more creative.

A brainstorming session has been had.

Memento wants to feed you to a mountain lion.
Little Fella wants to keep it strictly biblical and stone you.

LITTLE FELLA *nods with gusto.*

I said let's start with a spell in the tomb. Not one for the
spectators, but it gives us somewhere to go.
What's your profession?

VICTOR. A sommelier.

GRANDMA. Now why would a sommelier use language that'd make a pimp blush?

VICTOR....

GRANDMA. Pity you couldn't channel that silence with my sergeant. Mouthing off like that. A word to the wise, in future – if you have a future – don't even make eye contact with men like Memento. Any Nazi with prospects is in Europe. They only send animals to Africa. Understood?

Grunt if you understand.

VICTOR *grunts*.

Are you married?

VICTOR....

GRANDMA. Are, you, married?

VICTOR. Yes.

GRANDMA. Who's the lucky lady?

Beat.

What's her name?

Beat.

You're nervous, Germans soldiers have a reputation and here I am asking about your *missus*.

VICTOR....

GRANDMA. Don't fret, I'm an old woman. My groin still throbs but those salad days are over. Now I settle for supper and parlais.

VICTOR....

GRANDMA. I've suddenly got the itch. The itch for a night out. I usually start in a little bar, but after, where to go? The Jewish quarter is out of the question – I've have had to ban my own soldiers from entering. Such is their *appetite*.

GRANDMA *stares at* LITTLE FELLA, *who looks down at his feet.*

I've been made aware that your wife lives *outside* the Jewish quarter.

VICTOR....

GRANDMA. Tunisian women are modest, a knock on their door could offend. However, a Jewess, and if you live outside the quarter, I imagine a fairly sophisticated Jewess is likely to be more accustomed to a European mentality, not to mention cuisine.

Beat.

Give me her name and address, and you'll be dug out of this tomb instantly.

Beat.

Unless Youssef knows?

YOUSSEF. I don't.

Beat.

GRANDMA. Little Fella. Get the present

LITTLE FELLA *has taken a wooden box off the sleigh.*

Can you see Little Fella holding a present?

Say yes if you can see it.

VICTOR. Yes.

GRANDMA. Oooooooooooooooooo what's inside?

VICTOR....

GRANDMA. Would you like a clue?

VICTOR....

GRANDMA. 'Tall dark stranger, with an endearing speech impediment, seeks a friend for walks in the garden.'

VICTOR....

GRANDMA. Think of it like a crossword. Six letters.

VICTOR....

GRANDMA. Let's make this elementary. Forgive the paraphrasing – 'I once had four legs until I was condemned to crawl on my belly.'

VICTOR....

GRANDMA. Christ the heat has burnt out everyone's brains.

Little Fella place the present near Victor's face.

LITTLE FELLA *places the box next to* VICTOR*'s face*.

Post-coital the vipers had a snooze. Little Fella was able to draw on his pet-shop experience and install them in said box.

Beat.

Flash it open a second. Show Victor we're no longer dealing in metaphor.

LITTLE FELLA *flashes open the box*.
VICTOR*'s breathing changes*.

The boy in me wishes to see what'll happen if we let the vipers out.

Tell me your address and I'll contain my urges.

Youssef speak now or forever hold your peace.

YOUSSEF. I don't know where she lives.

Beat.

GRANDMA. Happy birthday.

GRANDMA *nods at* LITTLE FELLA.
LITTLE FELLA *walks towards* VICTOR. *Kneels down to open the box –*

1.2

NOVEMBER 1942… EARLY DAYS IN THE NAZI OCCUPATION… BEFORE THE BLONDS GOT SERIOUS.

A day at the beach, but not bathing-suit weather.

LOYS *sits rigid on a towel, eating sunflower seeds. Using her teeth alone she cracks open the shells, spits them out and swallows the seed.*

FAIZA *is lying on a towel, reading.*

LOYS. How's the book?

FAIZA. Mm.

   Beat.

LOYS. Is it something I'd like?

FAIZA. You can borrow it after.

   Beat.

LOYS. What's it about?

FAIZA. A cockroach.

You're chewing quite loudly.

LOYS *chews quietly.*

LOYS. I can see you becoming one of those people that walks around holding a book. Instead of carrying it in a bag, you'll walk around La Marsa just holding it. Emine does that doesn't she. Yesterday at the fishmonger's, she had her nose in something. Emine we get it. You read.

LOYS *returns to chewing loudly.*

FAIZA. Too many of those and you'll have to go home and poo.

LOYS. Inshalla. My insides are clenched up like a fist.

FAIZA. How long has it been?

LOYS. Months.

FAIZA. Shut-up months.

LOYS. And I've got these things in my bottom the size of grapes.

FAIZA....

LOYS. Cigarette?

FAIZA. A witch told me to stop if I want life in my womb.

LOYS. A witch?

FAIZA. My mum.

LOYS *lights up.*

LOYS. Is now the time for babies?

FAIZA. You can't coordinate babies with appropriate world events.

FAIZA *eyes up the cigarette.*
LOYS *lights one for her.*

LOYS. Victor and I tried last night.

FAIZA. I thought this wasn't the time.

LOYS. Perhaps that's why it didn't work.

FAIZA. He went soft?

LOYS. The opposite, he kept going and going.

FAIZA. Wow.

LOYS. I got bored.

FAIZA. A lot of pounding?

LOYS. Like he was trying to win a race.

FAIZA. Uh

LOYS. I still managed to climax.

FAIZA. *That* I envy.

LOYS. Faiza – the eye!

FAIZA *and* LOYS *gesture to ward off the evil eye.*

Victor turned blue, insisted on taking a cold bath.

FAIZA. You made love in the bath?

LOYS. Alone, he wanted to bathe alone.

FAIZA. Hardly a problem.

LOYS. Really.

FAIZA. My passion fucked off in January.

LOYS. Where did it go?

FAIZA. God never said.

LOYS. Wait so you haven't since January!?

FAIZA. Oh no, we were, but it always felt like maintenance. Until recently, something has changed. Ever since the Blonds appeared on the horizon I can't get enough. I'm waking Youssef most nights.

LOYS. Maybe you have Nazi ovaries.

FAIZA. God willing Youssef has Nazi balls. Have ourselves a gorgeous Nazi baby.

LOYS. Praise be.

A plane starts circling the beach.
FAIZA *and* LOYS *watch... bracing themselves.*

A pamphlet flutters down onto the sand.
FAIZA *and* LOYS *still size it up like it's a bomb.*

LOYS. What did the bank say?

FAIZA. They won't finance the rebuilding of the shop.

LOYS. Oh my love.

FAIZA. They said that we could apply for a different type of loan, so it's not (over)

LOYS. Habibti –

FAIZA. Something will show its face, I'm feeling optimistic.

LOYS. Okay but if it doesn't, you only have to ask.

FAIZA. Thanks.

LOYS. You'd do the same for / us.

FAIZA. Yes.

LOYS. Call it a loan if you prefer.

FAIZA. We're / fine.

LOYS. I'd love to help.

FAIZA. We don't need your money, habibti.

   Beat.

LOYS. Are you going to pick that up?

FAIZA. Why?

   Beat.

   LOYS *picks up the flyer.*

LOYS. These are getting better. (*Reading.*) We are friends to the Muslims.

   Beat.

FAIZA. Everyone sees through their bullshit.

LOYS. Do they.

FAIZA. Are you sleeping?

LOYS. Am I sleeping?

FAIZA. You seem grouchy.

LOYS. No I am not sleeping Faiza are you sleeping?

FAIZA. Nobody in Tunis is truly sleeping, but I found a way the other night, are you interested?

LOYS....

FAIZA. Stuff your ears with garlic.

LOYS. Okay.

FAIZA. Look it doesn't silence the booms, it doesn't stop the ground from shaking but the smell, sends me off.

LOYS. Poor Youssef.

FAIZA. He does the same, we sleep like cats.

LOYS. I barely cook with it, it's not going anywhere near me.

FAIZA. Then speak to Rene. She's got these sleeping pills from Casablanca. Black market stuff – expensive – but apparently these pills *really* put you out.

LOYS. (Okay.) I'm not eating, sleeping, shitting...

LOYS *scrunches up the pamphlet. Looks around. Unscrunches.* FAIZA *takes the pamphlet off her.*

FAIZA. You know that Italian shoe shop in Sidi Bou Said?

LOYS. Yeah.

FAIZA. Couple of years ago I went in. I was very nervous you know what I'm like in shoe shops, anyway a Sicilian guy comes to measure my feet, I tell him it's unnecessary, he insists, holds my foot and this current shoots through my body. I forget my feet that belong in the circus and the Sicilian fits me with the most exquisite winter sandals.

LOYS. Oh those.

FAIZA. *Yes those*. What I never told you, was that the following month I didn't sleep, eat or shit. Sicily had burned his way into me. It was torture. And bliss.

LOYS. Bet you wish something had happened.

FAIZA. (No.) I can keep the fantasies. What would be the reality...? Two minutes in a store cupboard, then Dad finding out, feeling like he *ought* to cut my head off.

LOYS. Still. What will it say on the wind as you travel to the next world? Here is Faiza... the girl who never took a risk.

FAIZA. Or. Here is Faiza. The girl who didn't need to fuck a greasy Sicilian to feel alive.

LOYS. Greasy now is he?

FAIZA. I'm lying to myself! He was a poem!

FAIZA *returns to her book.*

LOYS. We might leave.

FAIZA. Leave where?

LOYS. Tunis. You should too.

FAIZA. I should what.

LOYS. Think about leaving.

FAIZA. I'd go mad in the country.

LOYS. There are other places we could go.

FAIZA. Run away as a four?

LOYS. Would Youssef be up for it?

FAIZA. Sure.

LOYS. You're laughing at me.

FAIZA. Don't be ridiculous. What's going on?

LOYS. Nothing... (Do I really have to tell you!?)

FAIZA. What?

LOYS. At the baths. You saw it. I saw you *see it*.

FAIZA. See what?

LOYS. The painted words.

FAIZA. *That*. That's nothing new.

LOYS. It's not just that! It's the looks in the restaurants, in the salon –

FAIZA. The looks, what *looks*?

LOYS. ...I'm just not sure Tunisia is for me.

FAIZA. ...You're Tunisian.

LOYS. ...Shall we play rummy?

FAIZA. The Blonds don't want a future here.

LOYS. They're putting in a lot of effort with the locals.

FAIZA. Well they don't humiliate us like the French.

LOYS. Step out with them then, see how it goes.

FAIZA. It'll *go* until we can claim some control.

LOYS. Right.

FAIZA. The new Tunisia will need women like us.

LOYS. Habibti we were schooled for added value in the marriage market.

   Beat.

FAIZA. Where would you go?

LOYS. Got a few countries on my mind.

FAIZA. Every country has rotten fruit. You think the Libyans are all angels?

LOYS. I'm not going to Libya.

FAIZA. And Egypt? Those stuck-up Alexandrians, dripping in jewels, obsessed with camel's milk.

LOYS. I wouldn't go to an Arab country.

FAIZA. What do you mean 'Arab country'?

LOYS. A place where Arabs can throw a Jewish toddler on a cactus.

Beat.

FAIZA. That was an isolated incident.

LOYS....?

FAIZA. Do we know any other toddlers that have been thrown on cacti?

LOYS. Why are you diminishing / this?

FAIZA. I'm not diminishing –

LOYS. The little boy was impaled.

FAIZA. And the perpetrators should be shot.

LOYS. They've not even been arrested.

FAIZA. Take that up with the French.

LOYS. Why do you think they've escaped justice?

FAIZA. Why is this even a thing!? It's one gruesome incident, you've had years of attacks from the French.

LOYS. Yeah, and perhaps they've inspired the locals.

FAIZA. Whoa whoa whoa – have your friends or family ever been attacked by locals?

LOYS. Faiza you know, deep down you / know.

FAIZA. So that's a / no

LOYS. Some... Arabs... see an opportunity.

FAIZA. Sure, an opportunity to be doctors, lawyers, judges

LOYS. At the expense of who!?

FAIZA. You're okay with Europeans taking your jobs but god forbid Tunisians become professionals!?

LOYS. Let's play rummy.

FAIZA. I don't want to play rummy! You've mixed up who the enemy is.

LOYS. I expect violence from Europeans – not our neighbours!

FAIZA. Your neighbours invite you over at Eid.

LOYS. For how much longer?

FAIZA. What is this Loys?

LOYS. I keep thinking they're going to break into my house!

FAIZA. Who are they!? What is wrong with you!?

LOYS. My head is pounding – I've got a constant stream of thoughts – I can't turn off the thoughts – I lie awake all night – while Victor sleeps like a child – my head grows larger and larger spinning so fast it might come off.

FAIZA. ...That's called growing up.

LOYS. Uhh!?

FAIZA. The voice in my head has one phrase on repeat – 'Keep your eyes on the ground.' You're lucky.

LOYS wards off the evil eye.

You're so lucky to be you.

LOYS wards off the evil eye.

LOYS. I've even thought about going to Palestine.

Pause.

FAIZA. Remind me where that is again.

LOYS. Just above Egypt.

FAIZA. ...*Isn't that also an Arab country?*

LOYS. Yeah it's the last place on my list.

Beat.

FAIZA. If you're feeling anxious about our new occupiers, join the resistance. Stop eating seeds.

FAIZA kisses LOYS goodbye.

LOYS. Are you angry at me?

FAIZA. I have to go and see my aunt. It's not always about you.

LOYS. May god reward you and Youssef with abundance.

FAIZA. Right, yep, thanks. (*She exits*.)

LOYS *digs her feet into the sand.*

YOUSSEF *enters, holding four ice creams.*

YOUSSEF. Where is everybody?

LOYS. Your wife rushed off to see her aunt. Victor's not coming.

YOUSSEF *looks at the ice creams.*

I'm not hungry.

YOUSSEF. Yes you are.

YOUSSEF *hands* LOYS *an ice cream.*

LOYS. Which aunt is sick?

YOUSSEF. Aunt Dido. She's dying.

LOYS. I wish you long life.

YOUSSEF. Keep it. Everyone's cheering. Dido's one of those aunts that stuffs chillis in your mouth whilst giving you advice. Where's the mystical man of salt?

LOYS. At work.

YOUSSEF. Victor working on the sabbath?

LOYS. Something came up.

Beat.

I like strawberry.

YOUSSEF....mm...

Beat.

I think I prefer mint.

LOYS. I've never had mint before.

YOUSSEF. You have.

LOYS. I haven't.

YOUSSEF. Few months ago Victor brought us all mint. You loved it. Got a brainfreeze.

LOYS. Oh.

Why didn't you buy mint then?

YOUSSEF. They only had strawberry.

LOYS. Just today?

YOUSSEF. I think forever. From now on it's only strawberry.

LOYS. An ice-cream stand with one flavour... this country is going to the dogs.

Beat.

YOUSSEF. Are you scared?

LOYS....We're fine.

YOUSSEF *keeps his eyes on* LOYS.

Are you?

YOUSSEF. A bit.

Beat.

LOYS. I walk around our streets, and I keep looking back thinking someone is following me.
Then I worry it's all in my head. Faiza thinks I'm paranoid.

YOUSSEF....
What do you intend to do?

Beat.

LOYS. We'll have to leave.
(And that hurts.)

LOYS *looks out to sea.*

YOUSSEF. Would you like another ice cream?

LOYS. I'm okay.

YOUSSEF *sighs, starts licking the remaining two ice creams.*

LOYS *plays with her cigarette packet.*

YOUSSEF. I should get into smoking.

LOYS. Alright.

YOUSSEF. It's in vogue, isn't it?

LOYS. You wanna try one after your ice creams?

YOUSSEF. I think I'll stick to shisha.

LOYS. ...I'm too easily influenced. I saw a Bette Davis picture and went out and bought a pack of twenty.

YOUSSEF. It's a lot *cooler* than a shisha pipe.

LOYS. '*Cooler*'?

YOUSSEF. Means fashionable. In American.

LOYS. Is that a compliment?

YOUSSEF. I think for *them*.

LOYS. Oi.

YOUSSEF. You used to have a soft spot for America.

LOYS. So did you.

YOUSSEF. We haven't seen eye to eye since they flattened my shop.

LOYS. Oh don't hold that against them.

YOUSSEF *smiles.*

YOUSSEF (*about the ice creams*). God have mercy I'm really struggling.

LOYS (*dry*). Keep going, I believe in you.

Faiza tells me you've been managing to sell a few pieces from home.

YOUSSEF. People are still buying.

LOYS. Wonderful.

YOUSSEF. And the bank are very close to approving my loan, so it won't be long, until I'm back in a shop.

LOYS. That's great.

YOUSSEF *turns away from* LOYS *and looks out to sea.*

If the bank loan doesn't come through, we could loan you the money. If for whatever reason… you don't have to say anything now. Just, think about it. And if you did want to take it, I'd never look at you any differently. You must know that.

I think what you source, what you repair, it's special. And it is too important not to be shared with the whole city.

YOUSSEF *dabs an ice cream in* LOYS*'s face.*

Youssef!

YOUSSEF. That was gentle, you threw it in my face.

LOYS. What?! When!?

YOUSSEF. Many years ago you threw an ice cream at my face.

LOYS. I never.

YOUSSEF. The bullied remember.

LOYS. Rubbish, the bullied erase.

YOUSSEF. That's not my experience.

LOYS. The *bullies*, if they have a conscience, revisit.

YOUSSEF. And do you?

Beat.

LOYS. It was probably a way to talk to you.

Beat.

I should be off.

YOUSSEF. Yes.

Beat.

LOYS. See you next week – Victor will have dealt with his work stuff by then.

YOUSSEF. Aunt Dido will be dead – Faiza won't need to rush off.

LOYS *turns around to walk away.*

Has life turned out how you thought?

LOYS. (Bit of a question.)

YOUSSEF. (Too heavy?)

LOYS....
When I was young my parents would sit in the courtyard playing backgammon, drinking Boukha. Victor and I sometimes do that.

You?

YOUSSEF. I got lucky with Faiza.

LOYS. I'll say.

YOUSSEF. Although I know my cousin resented the lack of choice.

LOYS. He's got a face like a pomegranate, what did he expect?

YOUSSEF *smiles.*

YOUSSEF. My cousin was in love with someone outside of the community.

LOYS. You're blessed to have Faiza.

YOUSSEF. Yes.
Do you ever feel (lost)?

LOYS. Sometimes.
We're just waiting... aren't we?

YOUSSEF....for what?

LOYS....the British.

YOUSSEF. The British. And then?

LOYS. They might stay. They might not.

YOUSSEF. Having no control of our lives it isn't / fair.

LOYS. It isn't.

YOUSSEF....

When you're young, you start out thinking about all the lives you could lead, but then you make a choice... and... and you're shaped by that choice.

LOYS. You're still young.

YOUSSEF. I don't want to be haunted.

Beat.

LOYS. Make the most of the life you've chosen.

LOYS *and* YOUSSEF *stare at each other.*

A week later. FAIZA *and* VICTOR *enter the beach.*

FAIZA. Have you heard the new Hédi Jouini?

VICTOR. You're obsessed.

LOYS. He's special.

YOUSSEF. What's this?

LOYS. Hédi Jouini released a new song.

VICTOR. Another one.

FAIZA. Where's your heart habibi?

VICTOR. Certainly not with him.

YOUSSEF (*to* FAIZA). It's too eclectic for our Victor.

VICTOR. No, that's not / why

YOUSSEF. Too folksy?

VICTOR. No / no

LOYS. Yes!

VICTOR (*laughing*). I don't like this – I can see where / this is go–

FAIZA. Too romantic?

YOUSSEF. Yes / yes

VICTOR. It's the lute, I've never taken to a person who insists on getting out the lute at any given / moment.

YOUSSEF. This isn't one of your pals this is / Hédi Jouini.

VICTOR. It's totally derivative. If you were in Andalucía, you'd throw him a peso.

FAIZA. Listen to his tone! He's an original!

A plane flies over.

LOYS. You're wasting your breath, Hédi would need to have studied at a conservatoire in Paris for Victor to even consider his / music.

VICTOR. That is not fair! I am not a snob!

FAIZA *and* LOYS *and* YOUSSEF. Absolutely I You are I The worst.

VICTOR. You all need to tune into something other than Radio Tunis for once in your narrow lives.

FAIZA. I can change your mind.

LOYS *and* YOUSSEF. Don't bother I He's an ostrich.

FAIZA *sings 'Lioum Galitli Zine Zin' by Hédi Jouini.*

LOYS *joins in.*

YOUSSEF *joins in.*

VICTOR *shakes his head.*
Then joins in.
Darkness.
A week later.

YOUSSEF. The motion was about whether we cooperate. A
young guy stood up to oppose. He told the room that the
Blonds shouldn't be trusted – that one Blond in particular
had touched his wife –

FAIZA. Touched?

YOUSSEF. Yes… I don't…

FAZIA. Right.

YOUSSEF. For the husband to stand up and oppose – that took
courage, he was vulnerable, he required support, some
affirmation. I couldn't… I couldn't look in his eyes…and the
room, the Party, they laughed, and then they shouted him
down. They stood up, pointed their fingers and, and I stood
up and pointed and called him a liar, saying one anecdote
about one Blond shouldn't dictate the direction of the
Party… I want to believe these Blonds, their promises, our
own country, how many years, how many more years of
dependency… but the guy who opposed, he was shaking. He
was weak. I felt an urge to kick him…

Beat.

FAIZA. And then you came here?

Beat.

YOUSSEF. I thought the sea might have some answers.

Beat.

FAIZA. About the job?

YOUSSEF. Yes about the job – what else?

Beat.

FAIZA. You have to turn down the job.

YOUSSEF. Yes.

FAIZA. Take Loys's money.

YOUSSEF. Yes.

FAIZA. We can't eat sunshine.

YOUSSEF. No.

FAIZA. It's just a loan, we'll pay it back.

YOUSSEF. I can't take this.

FAIZA. Take what?

YOUSSEF. I can't take money from Loys. It isn't a pride thing... I just (can't)...

Beat.

FAIZA. Would you take from Victor? It's the same / money

YOUSSEF. It's not the same, and no I probably wouldn't.

FAIZA. Okay... but if it isn't pride...?

YOUSSEF. ....They'd never let us pay them back.

FAIZA. We'd insist.

YOUSSEF. They wouldn't accept.

FAIZA. How do you know?

YOUSSEF. Because if the situation was reversed and I had the means, I wouldn't let them pay me back.

FAIZA. Youssef... friends help...

YOUSSEF. I'm not taking their money.

FAIZA. Please don't hide from me.

YOUSSEF. I'm not hiding.

FAIZA. Why are you so closed?

YOUSSEF....

FAIZA. Do you think it's *manly*?

YOUSSEF....

FAIZA. To stand alone?

YOUSSEF. We have different visions of ourselves, different expectations.

FAIZA. Your visions are going to kill us. Any fool can say no. Who's brave enough to open their palm and look their benefactor square in the eye?

YOUSSEF. You'd feel worthless after.

FAIZA. Only if we squandered it. Not if we used it. Rebuild the business, make the second bedroom habitable, get ourselves into a position where we can actually raise a family.

YOUSSEF. Why should we take if we don't need?

FAIZA. We need we need we need what is the alternative?!

YOUSSEF. I take the job.

FAIZA. The *actual* alternative.

YOUSSEF. What's wrong with being a chef?

FAIZA. It depends on who you're cooking for.

YOUSSEF. Cooking is cooking, whether they're brown or blond.

Beat.

FAIZA. Youssef.

YOUSSEF. What?

FAIZA. You can't cook.

Beat.

YOUSSEF. You'll have to teach me.

Pause.

FAIZA. I expect to make sacrifices
    a degree of blindness
    only
    how much dignity could we lose?
    how filthy might it feel?

1.3

Twilight in the labour camp.
Heavy rain.
A floodlight orbits with menace.

YOUSSEF *holds an umbrella over* VICTOR*'s head.*

YOUSSEF. Eat the date.

    Beat.

    Victor.

    Beat.

    What would I tell Loys – He stopped eating!?

    Beat.

    Okay I'm placing the date in your mouth.

    VICTOR *turns his head away.*

    How many times – I sent a note to Faiza. She would have gone straight to collect Loys. The girls will be back at mine playing rummy as we speak. Now please have a date.

VICTOR. What if Loys was out when Faiza knocked on?

YOUSSEF. Then she'd search Tunis till she found her.

VICTOR. There are so many ways this could go wrong.

YOUSSEF. We're not going over this again!

VICTOR. Go to mine, make sure Loys isn't there.

YOUSSEF. She'll already be with Faiza.

VICTOR. Make sure!

YOUSSEF. If I leave, you'll drown.

VICTOR. You can be back in two hours.

YOUSSEF. Can you hold your breath for two hours?

Beat.

We wouldn't be in this situation if you'd just kept your mouth shut.

VICTOR. I saw snakes.

YOUSSEF. You thought you saw snakes.

Beat.

VICTOR. What's precious to you?

YOUSSEF. Victor –

VICTOR. Tell me, what's precious?

YOUSSEF....Faiza, my family.

VICTOR. Will rescuing Loys hurt your precious ones?

YOUSSEF. Loys doesn't need rescuing.

VICTOR. You have an opportunity to save a life, it's rare to be granted –

YOUSSEF. This is not an opera plot. Loys will be with Faiza!

VICTOR. What if she's not? Just imagine if she's not and he's he's there!

YOUSSEF. Okay if for some bizarre reason she's not / and

VICTOR. And Grandma knocks on her door!!

YOUSSEF. Grandma is not interested in women like that.

VICTOR. Old men aren't interested in young women now?

YOUSSEF. He wanted a home-cooked dinner, that's all, he's not like the others.

VICTOR. Whoever saves a life saves the world.

YOUSSEF. Please don't quote the Koran at me.

VICTOR. It's the Talmud.

YOUSSEF. That either.

VICTOR. I have some savings, Loys has her own savings, let us help!

YOUSSEF. This isn't about money – you're not hearing me – if I leave, you'll drown!

Beat.

VICTOR. I should have given another address.

YOUSSEF. It's okay, she'll be safe.

VICTOR. I've always had a big mouth.

YOUSSEF. You were scared.

VICTOR. You'd have done the same?

YOUSSEF. (No.) Yes.

VICTOR....My parents are gone and I don't like my sister. I can't lose Loys, I only have Loys I only have Loys.

YOUSSEF *checks the position of the orbiting light from the watchtower.*
Starts digging VICTOR *out of his hole.*

1.4

A version of LOYS *and* VICTOR*'s home if Salvador Dalí were to doodle it on the back of a napkin.*

Out of the earth rises up a ridiculously tall ticking grandfather clock.

There's a very long table shaped like a seesaw.

A tiny wooden door in the distance.

LOYS *stands rigid.*

GRANDMA. You drink red don't you?

   Beat.

   It's raining – I thought tonight's a *red* night.

   Beat.

   Lovely. Where are the glasses? Or should we just go at it like students?

   LOYS *gets out the glasses.*
   GRANDMA *pours.*
   They drink.

   How do you rate the grape?

LOYS....

GRANDMA. I don't know much about wine, do you?

LOYS....

GRANDMA. I can taste it when it's bad. This isn't bad. Not great. But certainly not bad.

LOYS. The safe is in the study, on the upper balcony.

GRANDMA. Is it?

LOYS. Would you like me to show you?

GRANDMA. I don't think so.

LOYS. There's a knack when opening, I'll need to show you.

GRANDMA. I'm not interested in your safe.

   Beat.

LOYS. Do you want the paintings?

GRANDMA. No, although I admire your taste.

LOYS. That one's real.

GRANDMA. I was going to say. It takes the breath away.

LOYS. Shall I fetch it down?

GRANDMA. I currently reside in a tent, it'll be fiddly to hang. What's for supper?

LOYS….

   Stew. Chicken stew

GRANDMA. Chicken in a stew! Marvellous! Any dips while we wait?

LOYS. Dips?

GRANDMA. Harissa? Bit of bread? I'm famished.

   LOYS *gets out some black bread and harissa sauce.*
   GRANDMA *dips.*

GRANDMA. Is it the uniform?

LOYS….?

GRANDMA. It's the uniform.

LOYS. Sorry?

GRANDMA. I understand why you can't see past it. That's precisely its point! Permit me to change, where's the bedroom? This way?

   GRANDMA *walks up the stairs and disappears.*

   LOYS *runs to the tiny door. It's locked.*

   She searches frantically for the keys. (They're on the table but she can't see them.)

   Rummages through her handbag.
   Takes out a box of pills.
   Pours some of the pills into the stew.
   GRANDMA *walks down the stairs, wearing a three-piece suit with a colourful tie and matching pocket square.*

LOYS *stirs the stew.*

How do I look?

LOYS....

GRANDMA. It's clearly intended for a younger man. Can I pull it off?

LOYS....

GRANDMA. Your husband is quite the dandy. Look at the tie! Where did he get it?

LOYS. I don't know.

GRANDMA. You don't buy his clothes?

LOYS. It was his wedding suit.

GRANDMA. I'm honoured. But will our marriage survive? Or will your temptress ways undo us. What a thrill. To be so close to Jewish heat.

Beat.

LOYS. Where are the keys?

GRANDMA. They're on the table.

LOYS....

GRANDMA. Such a bore isn't it. You lose your mind searching jackets not worn in years and all the while they're on the table. Exactly where you left them. Would you like me to rustle up a salad?

LOYS. I'm not feeling that well, I'm sorry, maybe we can arrange supper for tomorrow, would that be, I can go to the market and prepare whatever you like so tell me what you like I can cook I'm quite versatile –

GRANDMA. Breathe Loys breathe

LOYS. I've dreamt of killing Nazis.

GRANDMA. Would you like to talk about that?

LOYS. Please leave. Or or this will be your your your your your last night.

GRANDMA. My last night. Not a bad way to go. We're inside all snug. Don't you love being snug when it's raining outside? The cooking smells remind me of more innocent times... and yet I feel very present... absolutely in sync with what is happening right now. If this is my last night... I welcome it with outstretched arms.

GRANDMA *takes a seat at the head of the table*.

Come sit or I'll start behaving like a lonely old drunk.

LOYS *sits*.

(*About the suit*.) Victor has taste.

LOYS. You know Victor?

GRANDMA. We've met.

LOYS. How – how is he?

GRANDMA. I can hold my head up high. Do you find that? Clothes which make you feel good transform your posture?

LOYS. Victor is he –

GRANDMA. I never used to care. I thought bits of cloth, it's the underneath that counts, never judge a book by its cover et cetera et cetera but if I walk out this door wearing this suit, the world will see... well... what will they see?

LOYS....

GRANDMA. European... monied... or at least someone who spends on clothes. Assumptions will be made about my profession. They won't see a Nazi. It took me less than a minute to change into this suit. Is that how long it takes to reinvent oneself? Perhaps we should only judge books by their covers.

LOYS....

GRANDMA. It's going to be a tedious evening if I have to do all the talking.

LOYS. The stew should be ready.

GRANDMA. Marvellous!

LOYS *serves* GRANDMA.

You're not eating?

LOYS. I'm not hungry.

GRANDMA. Please join me.

LOYS. Can I wait a few minutes?

GRANDMA. Absolutely let's wait.

LOYS. You start, it'll go cold.

GRANDMA. Only if you're certain? I wouldn't want to offend?

LOYS. Start, please.

GRANDMA *goes to eat, hesitates.*

GRANDMA. Have you poisoned this?

LOYS. When would I have done that?

GRANDMA. Whilst I was changing into your husband.

LOYS. I'm not sure what you keep in your kitchen but –

GRANDMA. All sorts of household items can be used to the same effect.

LOYS. Then don't eat.

GRANDMA. It smells so good!

LOYS. So eat.

GRANDMA. You'll appreciate I can't trust you.

LOYS. I thought you welcomed death with outstretched arms.

GRANDMA. Means and ends, means and ends my dear. A bullet to the temple is a different story to poison. Poison can make you foam at the mouth and bleed from the eyes. In that respect it's similar to g(as).

GRANDMA *takes a mouthful.*

Bravo.

Leans back away from his bowl.

I've never had supper with a Jewess. I suspect you've never had supper with someone like me.

Beat.

I'm Grandma by the way.

LOYS *snorts*.

She laughs. A chink.

LOYS....

GRANDMA. I'm now sensing hostility.

LOYS....

GRANDMA. Aren't the Israelites famed for their hospitality?

LOYS....

GRANDMA. Abraham, aged ninety-nine, recently circumcised, runs, or more realistically hobbles out of his tent to invite the three angels to eat with him. The angels tell Abraham that god is going to destroy Sodom on account of there being no righteous men. Abraham argues. The angels say take it up with god. Abraham has a go defending the people but to no avail. God turns the whole of Sodom into salt. What an imagination. When I need ideas, I go straight to the Torah.

LOYS. How is Victor?

GRANDMA. He's building roads for a new Tunisia.

LOYS. Is he okay?

GRANDMA. He's more than okay. He's part of a great project.

LOYS. What project?

GRANDMA. Turning Tunisia into a country that can be ruled by Tunisians.

What do you think about that?

Beat.

LOYS. Am I obliged to speak?

GRANDMA. You're not obliged to do anything. But I have a frightening amount of authority. I might be able to help.

LOYS. Free my husband.

GRANDMA. Now hold on I'm not an anarchist.

LOYS. Will Victor be sent to Europe?

GRANDMA. Not if he behaves.

LOYS. Is he, behaving?

GRANDMA. There's room for improvement.

LOYS....

GRANDMA. I shan't take another mouthful of stew until you do.

> LOYS *eats a mouthful of stew.*
> GRANDMA *tucks in.*

I'll be seeing him tomorrow, I can pass on a message.

LOYS. Yes, let me go and write / something

GRANDMA. It needs to be spoken, I'm not the postman.

LOYS. Um, right, okay.

> Tell him, tell him, that I... I...
> To think about his operas.

GRANDMA. Don't lovers in the opera tend to die?

LOYS. He'll understand.

GRANDMA. Consider it done. Any messages for Youssef?

LOYS. Youssef?

GRANDMA. We both know who I'm talking about.

> *Beat.*

I suppose you can just tell him in person. He's such a good little Nazi I might start giving him an extra night off a week. Would that please you?

Beat.

LOYS. Would you like some more stew?

GRANDMA. Please.

LOYS serves GRANDMA more stew.

The Arabs are an enigma. They've yet to fully succumb to our charms in the same way that the Poles or the Romanians or the French or the Dutch or the Austrians or the Czechs or the Greeks or the Hungarians or the Latvians or the Lithuanians or the Italians or the Yugoslavians or the Luxembourgians *have* – but the Arabs… they won't show their hand.
I'm not concerned. Early days.

GRANDMA eats.

Madam Buonafaro it's criminal to be enjoying such a delicious stew alone. Eat.

LOYS takes another mouthful of stew.

Beat.

Lovely neighbourhood. Entirely different to the Jewish quarter. It's like we're in another country. Cities can be like that can't they?

Beat.

LOYS. One day the world will turn away from you.

GRANDMA. Do you think? Much of the world have taken us to their hearts.

LOYS. For now.

GRANDMA. What do you anticipate changing?

LOYS. They'll see through you.

GRANDMA. And what will they find?

LOYS. You're boring.

GRANDMA. Boring?

LOYS. You reduce everyone to one word.

GRANDMA. How so?

LOYS. Look there walks a *Jew*.

GRANDMA. We're distilling, not reducing.

LOYS. Whatever, it's boring. Nobody wants to be just one thing. They want to be many things.

GRANDMA. Who has the luxury to be many things?

LOYS. People who refuse the labels the world sticks on them.

GRANDMA. You talk from privilege Madam Buonafaro. Most people are forced to play the parts the world sees them in.

LOYS. You're not exactly helping matters.

GRANDMA. We're trying to define the essence of people.

LOYS. What do you know about my essence?

GRANDMA. You walk into a room and people learn you're a Jew. They might not shoot you, but they will reframe you. Every other way you describe yourself will be coloured with knowledge of your Jewishness. Understand we're not changing human nature, we're simply pointing out who people are.

LOYS. Is that why you need the yellow stars?

GRANDMA. We stole that little idea from the Arabs.

LOYS. They didn't use it to hurt us.

GRANDMA. Are you not a Jew?

LOYS. What if I'm more of a birdwatcher than a Jew?

GRANDMA. I suspect your Jewishness ranks higher than your twitching.

LOYS. How can you possibly know!?

GRANDMA. Okay, okay, little hypothetical question, if you were to be reborn in the next minute would you come back as a Jew?

LOYS. No, there's a Nazi in my kitchen.

GRANDMA. Putting that aside for one moment.

LOYS. I might come back as a lion.

GRANDMA. A Jewish lion?

LOYS. Are you always this annoying?

GRANDMA. I'll wager that you'd experiment with every single aspect of yourself, except your Jewishness.

LOYS. Would you still come back as a Nazi with bad breath?

GRANDMA *whips out a breath spray.*

GRANDMA. I might come back as a Jew. I'm already trying it for size.

LOYS. So you knock on my door, for what? A practice? A test?

GRANDMA. Joy, I'm looking for joy.

LOYS. Why did you become a Nazi!?

GRANDMA. I went to a rally – I liked his charisma.

LOYS. What about the content!?

GRANDMA. Nobody's perfect, but the Party, I was sucked in by its gravitational pull. It chose me. Surely you can understand that feeling. How special it is to feel *chosen*? To be part of a team, to have a connection with strangers, the warmth of belonging.

LOYS. So join a fucking netball team.

GRANDMA. Well yes, in lieu of political expression, see competitive sports.

Beat.

LOYS. Before you came... I was... many things. I worked in the wine business. Sung in a choir. Went to the steam baths, talked shit in the salon – and yes, I'm Jewish, but if you stick a yellow star on me, everything else I am or could be... evaporates.

GRANDMA. Why are you worrying about yellow stars? Your people barely adhere to them. It's a means of identification. We thought you all had horns.

LOYS. How frustrating.

GRANDMA. Stars enable my less-enlightened subordinates to spot you.

LOYS. Are you thirsty?

GRANDMA. I'm enjoying the wine.

LOYS. Fancy some blood?

GRANDMA. Pardon?

LOYS. I've got a Christian baby chained up in the basement.

GRANDMA. Funny, very funny, but then you Jews are – you have to be.

LOYS. Is this your idea of a night out?

GRANDMA. I'm having a good time.

LOYS. You look awful in that suit.

GRANDMA. I beg your pardon.

LOYS. Like a camel with tumours.

GRANDMA. Don't hold back.

LOYS. What will you do after the war?

GRANDMA. Go to the pub.

LOYS. Who with?

GRANDMA. Like-minded people.

LOYS. That'll be fun, a pub where everybody thinks the same.

GRANDMA. Madam Buonafaro you're failing to recognise the experimental nature of our project. Part of the world tells us that we should embrace people of different hues. That diversity enriches a culture. My Führer is simply trying out another model. He takes the family as an example. Children from different parents could live together happily, there are many cases of happily adopted orphans, but a better recipe for happiness is children born by the same parents living under one roof.

LOYS. Are you going to kill me?

Beat.

GRANDMA. Eat.

LOYS *pushes away the bowl.*

Beat.

It's never my intention to kill. I'm actually a Zionist.

LOYS. Oh my god.

GRANDMA. And I'm not the only Nazi Zionist. You've got cheerleaders in all sorts of corners. Even the Führer, in his own, special way.

LOYS. Stop stop –

GRANDMA. I suppose Zionism shares something with Nazism – in its commitment to purity.

LOYS. It shares nothing with –

GRANDMA. Thought we'd find common ground on Zionism.

LOYS. You're not a Zionist.

GRANDMA. Jews yearn for their own homeland – how would you define it?

LOYS. You are not a / Zionist.

GRANDMA. Quite similar to *Lebensraum*.

LOYS *puts her face in her hands.*

Isn't it time? I mean by god you deserve it. How many years have you been watching your neighbours burn down your houses, smash your shops, evict you, traipse from one country to the next, ghetto to ghetto. Are you not the people without a land? Destined for the land without a people?

LOYS. You've taken a special idea and corrupted it.

GRANDMA. Nobody owns an idea.

LOYS. Never said we owned, but your association... dirties...

GRANDMA. Ideas are not clean or dirty, they're wild, Zionism in particular, it's about as concrete as a dream.

Perhaps you're not really a Zionist? When it comes down to it. Perhaps you prefer the persecution. Prefer to feel special? On the brink of extinction. Hanging on. While the rest of the world settles for remaining invisible... the Jew screams 'Look at me, look at me, hanging off the edge of the cliff!!'

LOYS. You talk a lot.

GRANDMA. It's my way of thinking... thinking aloud... a word articulates a thought... forget the word and you forget the thought. Take the word *Jew*. Without the word, the Jew no longer exists.

LOYS. Just stop talking about us then.

GRANDMA. You talk too much about yourselves.

LOYS. So don't listen!

GRANDMA. I try not to, you make such good films.

LOYS. This is exhausting!

One minute you say you need a system like yellow stars to make the Jew visible – the next minute you say the Jew is unwilling to be invisible. Why don't you go and find a cave and arrive at something coherent before you waste any more of my fucking time.

Beat.

GRANDMA. Watch it Loys.

LOYS. You watch it, *Grandma*.

What's your real name?

GRANDMA. To you I'm Grandma.

LOYS. Is it embarrassing?

GRANDMA. It's very ordinary. The boys came up with Grandma. In the evenings I knit for them. One called me

Grandma. At first I was offended but then I thought this is my get-out-of-jail card. If by some miracle the British win, they'll want heads to roll. Who was the psycho in charge of the Tunisian camps? Good luck finding Grandma.

LOYS. You refer to yourself as a psycho?

GRANDMA. I'm working on self-acceptance. Any coffee?

LOYS *makes coffee.*

(*In a southern Yankee drawl.*) Add a splash of orange blossom like them Arabs do.

Pause.

LOYS. Knitting for the *boys* hey?

GRANDMA. I find it a real switch-off.

Beat.

LOYS. Are you married?

GRANDMA. I was.

LOYS. Did she leave you?

GRANDMA. It was a mutual decision.

LOYS. Who instigated the conversation?

GRANDMA. Nobody instigated – it was a / mutual

LOYS. She get bored too?

GRANDMA....

LOYS *serves the coffee.*

GRANDMA *drinks his coffee.*

I don't have the words to describe this taste. Perhaps if I spend some more time here I might find them. Yes, that's a resolution. After the war, regardless of outcome, I'll give Tunisia a whirl.

LOYS. Think you can walk away after this scot-free?

GRANDMA. Absolutely.

LOYS. I know your face I won't forget your face.

GRANDMA. Then I best gouge out your eyes.

Beat.

GRANDMA*'s eyes stay locked on* LOYS.

Undoes his tie and a couple of shirt buttons.

Any sweets?

LOYS *slides over box of Turkish delight.*

Oh my.

Are these from Youssef?

LOYS....(what?)

GRANDMA. Yes... yes... never simple is it?

LOYS....

GRANDMA. Who we love.

GRANDMA *eats Turkish delight and stares at* LOYS.

...I was in love with someone else. I should have had the courage to leave the marriage, before the children... build a life with the woman I truly (loved). Madam Buonafaro. You've got me all worked up.

GRANDMA *falls asleep.*

LOYS *hyperventilates.*
Composes.

Stares at the sleeping GRANDMA, *with steel in her eyes.*

Intermission.

2.1

LOYS *and* VICTOR*'s riad.*

A mixture of sandstone, marble and mosaic. The space possesses a crumbling grandeur, a woozy magic.

The courtyard is circled by soft furnishings, brightly patterned cushions and incense candles.
In the centre is the sahridj (fountain).
Dotted around the courtyard are citrus trees and jasmine.

Off the central courtyard are doors leading to bayts (elongated rooms) such as the kitchen and dining area. We can make out the grandfather clock from the previous scene.
Upstairs is the balcony floor with doors leading off to the bedrooms, the study, etc....

The rain has stopped, the stars are out.

LOYS, *sweating, exits a balcony room, walks down the stairs, clutching a bag.*

FAIZA *is standing in her courtyard. She holds a key.*

FAIZA. I knocked.

LOYS. I didn't hear.

> *Beat.*

FAIZA. Lucky, I still have this. Can't even remember when you gave it to me.

> Found it under a pillow.

Would you like it back?

LOYS *shakes her head.*

Here, I don't need it.

LOYS. Keep it.

FAIZA. I don't want the responsibility.

LOYS. It's late Faiza.

FAIZA. I couldn't sleep. All night I can't sleep.

LOYS. I was just heading out for a walk.

FAIZA. Clear your mind.

LOYS. Yeah.

FAIZA. What's up?

LOYS. What?

FAIZA. What do you need to clear?

LOYS. Nothing in particular.

Beat.

I thought if I worked up a sweat – it's what you're doing isn't it?

FAIZA. In a way. Although I don't go out with a bag.

LOYS. *This.*

FAIZA. You've overstuffed it.

LOYS. It's very old.

FAIZA. Type of bag you'd take if you were running away but didn't want to look like you were running away.

LOYS. You spent too many hours at the pictures.

FAIZA. That'll be it. Silly me.

Beat.

LOYS. All Jews have their bags packed. I wasn't taking it out on my walk.

FAIZA. Where were you planning to walk?

LOYS. You working for the Gestapo now?

Beat.

FAIZA. Is that where your mind goes?

LOYS. It was a joke.

FAIZA. They pay their informants well. Look you in the eye. I'd no longer be invisible. Or in your shadow.

LOYS. Have you been smoking kief?

FAIZA. Where do you walk at night? And with who?

LOYS. …I walk alone. Around La Marsa.

FAIZA. So do I, I never see you.

LOYS. I don't often go your way. Sometimes I walk to Carthage.

FAIZA. If I was to rip open your blouse, would I find all your jewellery around your neck.

LOYS. …What's happening habibti?

FAIZA. What, I can't surprise my old friend?

Beat.

LOYS. Walk to the beach with me.

FAIZA. Not at this time.

Beat.

I got a note from Youssef saying I should save you from a night on your own – invite you over immediately.

LOYS. 'Save me from a night on my own…'?

FAIZA. Do you need saving?

LOYS. Do I look in need of saving?

FAIZA. Hard to tell. You could be trapped in a burning building, I'm not sure you'd play the damsel.

LOYS. I'd jump. When did you get the note?

FAIZA. This afternoon.

LOYS. Uh.

Beat.

FAIZA. I couldn't bring myself to come over this afternoon. Then I found this key and (thought I'll surprise you). The note… I thought Youssef might be coming home, although tonight isn't his night off, but the note, maybe he wanted us all to (talk). Anyway. He didn't come home. I've not seen him for twelve days.

LOYS. Victor has been gone three months.

FAIZA. Do you miss him?

LOYS. (How can you even ask me that!??)

Beat.

FAIZA. Whatever you've done, I'm willing to look beyond it.

LOYS….

FAIZA. If you need help, if you're in any type of trouble?

Beat.

LOYS. Faiza it's time for you to leave.

FAIZA. Youssef is not the man I settled for, he's the man I love. Our home may not be Eden, but it'll serve as long as we watch out for serpents.

LOYS. Why are you speaking Arabic, we never / speak

FAIZA. What might you betray if you speak a little Arabic?

LOYS. I prefer French.

FAIZA. Speaking French makes me sick
and for this announcement
my mother tongue best fits.
There is life in me.

LOYS....All my blessings. A thousand blessings.

FAIZA. Goodbye Loys.

LOYS. Faiza.

FAIZA. Go far away.

LOYS. Faiza.

FAIZA. I don't know how our lives turned out like this, I could never have predicted (this). When we were children I thought I was a descendent of Kahina. I'd prophesise… what Mum would make for lunch, how long Dad would bathe his feet in sea salts – small stuff – not the size of armies or what direction they would come, but still, enough for me to believe I had some Kahina in me. I always thought you'd be here, always thought we'd be close.

LOYS. Habibti…

FAIZA. Go where you need to,

LOYS. Let me at least,

FAIZA. But go alone.

LOYS. Hug you…

FAIZA. If you take him, I'll raise an army.

FAIZA *exits*.

LOYS *sits*.

Picks up the bag, walks towards the front door, opens –
LITTLE FELLA *IS STANDING ON THE THRESHOLD*.
LOYS *screams*. LITTLE FELLA *puts a hand to her mouth*.

LITTLE FELLA. Where's Grandma?

LOYS. He's upstairs.

LITTLE FELLA. Oh. *Oh*. You must have really put on the charm offensive.

LOYS. Yes.

LITTLE FELLA. Just saw a local leave here and I thought oi oi what's all this.

LOYS. She's my maid. Came to clear away the supper.

Beat.

LITTLE FELLA. Mind if I take a look upstairs?

LOYS. …I don't think that would be appropriate do you?

LITTLE FELLA. Depends on what's going on.

LOYS. We've been having a lovely time… but my instinct is… the evening has not yet finished.

LITTLE FELLA. Gotcha. I was worried you'd killed him.

LITTLE FELLA *walks around.*

LOYS. I should be getting back to / Grandma

LITTLE FELLA. No harm in making a man wait. Let him recharge. He's not young like us.

Beat.

It's very quiet in here.

LOYS. The beauty of this architecture. You can't hear what's going on outside.

Beat.

LITTLE FELLA. You know what for my own peace of mind I need to go upstairs and have a look –

LOYS. Okay I killed him.

LITTLE FELLA. What?

LOYS *picks up a knife.*

LOYS. Not easy cutting a man up, but I persevered, and then I popped him in the stew.

LITTLE FELLA. You what?

LOYS. I ate him! I was hoping he might act as a laxative, but at the moment he's sitting very heavy. Shouldn't be surprised. He's all stodge!

LITTLE FELLA *laughs*.
The laughs die.

LITTLE FELLA. What happens when you die?

LOYS....

LITTLE FELLA. The lads outside all had theories.

LOYS. What lads?

LITTLE FELLA. I was too shy say mine.

LOYS....

LITTLE FELLA. I die. Open my eyes. I'm up a mountain. Snowy in the winter. Daisies in the summer. At the top of this mountain, there's a cabin. It's made of... wood. Got a chimney, and from miles and miles you can see the smoke rising. I'll admire the cabin for a while, the workmanship's pukka. But there's only so long you can admire the outside of somewhere. I'll open the door. It's full of people. Everyone is welcome. Girls. Men. Women. Children. Grandmas – not (him upstairs) – real grandmas, the ones obsessed with soap... All the people gather around the fire and play board games. When it's sunny, we go for walks, hunt rabbits – if we're lucky, wild boar. The best thing about this cabin is that new people arrive every day, and yet somehow it never gets too full. Someone is always telling a funny story and cos nobody knows each other we're always on our best behaviour.

LOYS....Right.

LITTLE FELLA. You should think about yours before the night's out.

Beat.

LOYS. My maid forgot to take out the rubbish. Actually if you're on your way out, would you mind taking it to the municipal bin across the street?

Beat.

LITTLE FELLA *picks up the bag.*

LITTLE FELLA. We'll be waiting outside. Memento invited every Nazi in Tunis for a piss-up on your corner! I love a get-together but between the beers and the weaponry, I do fear the night will end in tears.

See you later.

LITTLE FELLA *exits.*

LOYS *crumples, finds the Turkish delight.*
Eats.

A sound.

Another sound – it's coming from the upstairs balcony. This is getting ridiculous!

LOYS. (What the fuck!?)

LOYS *hides in a shadowy alcove at the back.*

Down the stairs from the upper balcony walks... VICTOR, *holding a rock.*

VICTOR *explores the downstairs rooms.*

Kneels by the water fountain, splashes water on his face.

From behind, LOYS *approaches with the knife.*

LOYS. Who's there?

VICTOR....
  Loys?

LOYS. Victor?

VICTOR. It's me.

LOYS. I didn't recognise you.

VICTOR. I've had a haircut.

LOYS....

VICTOR. Been on a diet.

LOYS....

VICTOR. Although all things considered, I actually look fairly decent.

LOYS. Come closer, let me look at you in the light.

Pause.

VICTOR. You're doing that thing when you look at me funny.

LOYS. What thing?

VICTOR. It happened when I came back from Tuscany... you looked at me funny.

LOYS. I don't remember that.

VICTOR. Like you don't know me.

LOYS. Must be shock.

VICTOR. Like you're seeing me, for the first (time)

LOYS. Sorry.

VICTOR. No, it's, nice.

Beat.

LOYS. Your skin...

VICTOR. The camp... it was quite outdoorsy.

LOYS. Right.

VICTOR. I got a tan, you dislike me with a tan?

LOYS. I don't.

VICTOR. And unshaved –

LOYS. Victor –

VICTOR. I look like a Bedouin salesman, groping in the darkness late…

LOYS. A bit of Rumi?

VICTOR. Just a bit.
I've imagined this moment.

LOYS. You're here now.

Beat.

VICTOR. You look pretty.

LOYS. (Hardly.) My hair is full of grease.

VICTOR. I like it. At the wedding it was curled up very high and you looked… otherworldly. I thought how will I cope day to day. Then Monday came and you were wearing a shit blouse and greasy hair… and I thought you even more spectacular.

Beat.

LOYS. Did the Nazis release you?

VICTOR. Why would you think that?

LOYS. On the radio it said they were losing control.

VICTOR. I escaped.

LOYS. …well done.

VICTOR. 'Well done'?

LOYS. Sorry, I…

Beat.

VICTOR. Are you disappointed?

LOYS. Victor?

VICTOR. You're not exactly jumping into my arms.

LOYS. Sorry, it's just, we've been bombed most nights, I've not had time to breathe.

VICTOR....
What's in the bag?

LOYS. Jewellery, clothes, francs.

VICTOR. You were leaving?

LOYS. The bag has been packed for three months, with your things too. For when you returned.

Beat.

VICTOR. Let's go then, let's leave Tunis.

LOYS. Now?

VICTOR. Yes Loys now. Out the back. While it's still dark.

LOYS. We could go to Abdul-Wahab's farm – there are Jewish families hiding there.

VICTOR. Where I'm thinking we don't need to do any hiding.

Beat.

From the pit of decay and dust,
With blood and sweat
Shall arise a race
Proud, generous and fierce,
Captured Betar, Yodfat, Masada,
Shall arise again in all their strength and glory.

LOYS. I wasn't part of those Zionist youth movements.

VICTOR. I used to think only a simpleton would take that song literally... would actually want to go there...

LOYS. Well you can't. They took the car.

VICTOR. I can get us a car.

LOYS. Let's spend a few days on this farm, consider our next steps –

VICTOR. I want us to be safe – and in the holy land –

LOYS. What do we even know about the holy land?

VICTOR. It'll be an adventure.

LOYS. You think it'll be the Garden of Eden?

VICTOR. (No.) It'll be a swamp, but it's *our swamp*.

LOYS. You sound like a fanatic.

VICTOR. What's going on Loys?

LOYS. I want to live somewhere… where I can be…
anonymous.

VICTOR. *Anonymous?*

LOYS. …somewhere quiet… where I can be… whoever I want
to *be*.

VICTOR. Is that a song lyric?

LOYS. *Victor.*

VICTOR. We can only be who we want to be with other Jews.

LOYS. We moved out of the quarter because we didn't like
other Jews!

Beat.

VICTOR. You'd rather stay here.

LOYS. Maybe not *here* here, but in this country.

VICTOR. I see.

LOYS. Our lives were once good.

VICTOR. Is that why you want to stay?

LOYS. Were our lives not good?

VICTOR. They were, and then the Blonds came, and you
started eating cuttlefish.

Beat.

LOYS. So I ate some cuttlefish.

Beat.

VICTOR. Is that all you ate?

   Beat.

   Betrayal comes in many shapes.

LOYS. I haven't betrayed you.

VICTOR. No?

LOYS. You betrayed *me*.

VICTOR....?

LOYS. Neglected me.

VICTOR. I've been in a camp.

LOYS. Before.

VICTOR. How?!

LOYS. Always talking, never listening.

VICTOR. I listen, I'm an excellent listener.

LOYS. Staying up late to lecture me about European music.

VICTOR. We stayed up late together.

LOYS. I didn't want to always stay up.

VICTOR. You never said.

LOYS. You never asked.

   Beat.

VICTOR. I thought doing jigsaws, listening to new music, I
   thought you were having fun.

LOYS. I was.

VICTOR. I can't remember you laughing...

LOYS. I never laugh out loud much.

VICTOR. Yes you do, with others.

LOYS. Do you want me to fake it?

VICTOR. I make everyone laugh.

LOYS (*flat*). You do, you're very funny.

Beat.

VICTOR. A few days before I was taken I woke you in the middle of the night – remember. I said let's just get out of Tunis head down south, hide out, just in case they come for me. And you said 'Go to sleep, only poor Jews are being sent to the camps.' I wonder... I wonder.

LOYS. (How dare you.)

A sound from upstairs.

VICTOR. Relax it's Youssef.

LOYS. He's here?!

VICTOR. How do you think I escaped.

LOYS. Shouldn't he go to Faiza?

VICTOR. We already stopped at hers. She wasn't in.

YOUSSEF *walks downstairs into the courtyard. He's bleeding from his side.*

LOYS....

YOUSSEF....

VICTOR. Where did you hide the horse?

YOUSSEF. Behind the bakery, or what was the bakery.

VICTOR. What is it now?

YOUSSEF. Rubble.

VICTOR. That's a fairly exposed place to hide a white horse.

YOUSSEF. It must be two kilometres away – they can't trace it back to *here*. Where's Grandma?

LOYS. What?

Beat.

YOUSSEF. There is a busload of Nazis waiting at the bottom of your street to drive an officer back to camp.

LOYS. Faiza dropped by earlier.

   I hear congratulations are in order.

YOUSSEF....thank you.

VICTOR. Who'd believe it – Youssef a dad.

LOYS. Yes.

VICTOR. Did you girls do the string test?

LOYS. We didn't. All my blessings. What happened to your side?

YOUSSEF. Just a scratch.

VICTOR. Before your imagination runs away from you, it's not a stab wound or a gunshot, nothing heroic like that, poor old Youssef just got his shirt caught on some wire.

LOYS. It could still be infected.

YOUSSEF. I'm fine.

LOYS. Don't be such a martyr.

   LOYS *exits into one of the bayts.*

VICTOR. Maybe he never showed.

YOUSSEF. What about all the soldiers?

VICTOR. They could be waiting for any officer.

YOUSSEF. His men drop him off, he has supper, then he leaves.

VICTOR. Perhaps Loys killed him.

YOUSSEF. Be serious.

VICTOR. I am!

YOUSSEF. Loys isn't a killer.

   LOYS *enters with a bottle of Boukha and a medical kit.*

LOYS. Why don't we all go into the kitchen it's getting cold out here.

VICTOR. Don't be daft, it's gorgeous.

Beat.

LOYS. You're better at these things habibi. Why don't I go and prepare you both some food?

VICTOR. Loys – patch him up.

LOYS *begins to attend to* YOUSSEF*'s wound.*

LOYS. It's bleeding a fair bit.

YOUSSEF. What do you propose?

LOYS. I could try and stitch it up.

YOUSSEF. Okay.
Do you know how to do that?

LOYS. I can sew a button.

YOUSSEF....

LOYS *starts to stitch up* YOUSSEF.

VICTOR *takes a swig of Boukha, stares at the two of them.*

VICTOR. Got steady hands, hasn't she?

YOUSSEF. Mm.

VICTOR. Steady, and yet... delicate.

LOYS. Be quiet I'm trying to concentrate.

VICTOR. Long fingers, piano player's fingers. A perfect, a perfectly proportioned hand. You could be a hand model Loys. Thirty years from now, when they're covered in liver spots, people would still pay for those hands.

Are you enjoying that?

LOYS. Pardon.

VICTOR. Attending to the wound.

LOYS. Happy for you to take over!?

Pause.

VICTOR. Perhaps in our new life you can train as a nurse. Where we're going they'll need nurses.

LOYS. It'll be a treat to prepare food for someone else. It's been a long time. What do you fancy?

VICTOR. We're not hungry.

LOYS. Youssef?

VICTOR. A chef is never hungry.

LOYS. Youssef can answer for / himself.

VICTOR. Should have seen the meals he cooked whilst we were camping. Ate like the beys didn't we? I've struggled to put on the weight, I must have worms or something, but Youssef, he's filled out, look at his cheeks, flushed and healthy, cuts a fine figure nowadays doesn't he Loys?

YOUSSEF. I'll eat something after.

VICTOR. When we were boys he was obsessed with prostitutes, but then he struck gold with Faiza, and that was the end of it, wasn't it?

YOUSSEF. Give it a rest.

VICTOR. What a shame you didn't come into your looks earlier. You could have had the pick of the town when the town was free and single –

LOYS. If we were to drive across Libya, could we stop at your cousins', get their advice on which roads to take, avoid...?

YOUSSEF. There are Nazis in Libya, where are you heading?

LOYS. Israel.
Stay still.

Pause.

There.

How does that feel?

VICTOR. Looks sewn up to me.

LOYS. Youssef?

YOUSSEF. Yep.

LOYS. It's stopped bleeding.

VICTOR. It has. Well done Loys. What a marvel you are.

YOUSSEF. Why would you go there?

VICTOR. Safety in numbers.

YOUSSEF. You'd feel safer in New York.

VICTOR. New York's pricey.

YOUSSEF. There are other places where you'd be safe – what about Abdul-Wahab's farm. You could be there in three hours. The Blonds won't bother you down there – they're too busy trying to control Tunis. Loys, you've heard about Abdul-Wahab's farm haven't you?

LOYS. I feel drawn to Palestine.

YOUSSEF. You've never been.

LOYS. Still, I long for it.

YOUSSEF. How can you long for somewhere you don't know?

LOYS. There's no sense to it.

YOUSSEF. Try, try and make sense!

LOYS. Why? If it feels right.

YOUSSEF. Because if you're going to the extremes of leaving your home, risking your life to travel across a continent at war, analyse your fucking feelings.

VICTOR. What's it to you!?

YOUSSEF. All I'm saying is… (*Stealing a look at* LOYS.) consider all your feelings… before you elevate one.

LOYS. We're leaving.

YOUSSEF. Home is more than just a place.

VICTOR. Don't make me vomit, I need all the stomach acid I can get.

YOUSSEF. Is your heart actually set on Palestine?

LOYS. Where else should we go? Italy was our home until it wasn't, Hungary was our home until it wasn't, Portugal was our home until it wasn't, Spain was our home until it wasn't, Russia was our home until it wasn't, Germany was our home until it wasn't, France was our home until it wasn't, Tunisia was our home...

YOUSSEF. It's still your home!

LOYS. Maybe... or maybe it has revealed something we always knew, only we pushed it so far into the back of our minds we thought it had gone away. We're guests in this country.

YOUSSEF. You've been here for hundreds of years.

LOYS. We've been *guests* in other people's homes for thousands of years! And we're good guests, we bring gifts, take off our shoes at the door, sing for our supper, help with the washing-up, but there comes a point in the evening when the hosts say enough is enough. It's 5 a.m. I want to go to bed with my own family in my own home – can you stop talking – can you stop asking questions – just... fuck off. After two thousand years we finally got the message. We're fucking off... back to our own home.

YOUSSEF. (Why are you angry at *me*?!)

LOYS. (Why am I angry at you!?!)

VICTOR. You'll love it when you get there.

YOUSSEF. You cannot go!

VICTOR. What business is it of yours?

YOUSSEF. There are people already living there.

LOYS. The Palestinians are about as Palestinian as we are Tunisian.

VICTOR. Don't wind him up.

LOYS. It's not a wind-up – you can live somewhere hundreds of years and it still isn't home.

YOUSSEF. So what – you remove them?

LOYS. Of course / not!

VICTOR. Don't talk stupid!

LOYS. We'll all just have to share.

YOUSSEF. How can you be so blind Loys?

VICTOR. What the fuck is it to you?

YOUSSEF. This is is is is Europe's crime – they should pay – they should give you... Valencia!

VICTOR. And eat tapas!? All those shitty little plates!?

YOUSSEF. Can the hungry choose?

VICTOR. Oh fuck a dog Yus – there are whole chunks of Palestine uninhabited.

YOUSSEF. I've seen a photo. The port was as busy as ours.

VICTOR. Yeah but the land is arid, it requires cultivation.

YOUSSEF. In the photo it looked green and lush.

VICTOR. Some Jewish settlers have started growing oranges.

YOUSSEF. You don't need to be Jewish to work out how to grow oranges. And how do you know who is growing what!? *You've never been!*

VICTOR. *We know people who've been.*

YOUSSEF. I know everyone you know!

VICTOR. What was the name of your cousin, the tall one, he went?

LOYS. Felix talked about it but then he decided on Cape Town.

VICTOR. Okay, well, we'll be the first Tunisians off the boat.

YOUSSEF. It's so far away.

VICTOR. Why do you care!?

YOUSSEF. Because… (*Stealing a look at* LOYS.) because… there is a myth… a myth that Palestine is some backwater, awaiting your *industry* – but you won't believe the amount of newspapers the Constitutionalists Party receives. Every Palestinian must be a journalist!

VICTOR. So they can read and write! Habibi, never until this night have you mentioned Palestine!

YOUSSEF. Neither have you!

LOYS. We're going. Will you drive us there?

YOUSSEF. (My love what are you doing?!)

VICTOR. We don't need a driver.

LOYS. If Youssef drives we look less like two Yids on the run.

YOUSSEF. What happens to me after I've miraculously delivered you?

LOYS. …Stay.

VICTOR. And leave Faiza!?

LOYS. Bring her with.

YOUSSEF. Now you want to risk Faiza's life too?

VICTOR. And the new baby!

LOYS. Well you'd never do the dishonour of leaving them, would you?

YOUSSEF. …

VICTOR. Youssef is not going to uproot his family for a shithole full of journalists.

YOUSSEF. Does calling it a shithole make it easier to colonise?

VICTOR. How can you say that?

YOUSSEF. Because if you go there, with your intention, you are no better than the French.

VICTOR. What intention!? We just wanna live!

YOUSSEF. Then go to the countryside! Like everyone else!

LOYS. In the country Jewish women are hiding down wells. Is that what you'd have me do? Hide and *pray* the patrols are made up of Nazi eunuchs.

YOUSSEF.…

LOYS. There's nothing for you here either.

YOUSSEF. (What are you actually asking me?)

LOYS. (Come with me.)

Beat.

VICTOR. I'm shivering.

LOYS. Let me feel.

…you're running a fever.

VICTOR. Just my luck, escape the camp, die of a cold.

LOYS. Why don't you go and lie down.

VICTOR.…

VICTOR *rises slowly.*

Will you come with?

LOYS. Yes. Of course.

Beat.

LOYS *and* VICTOR *start to climb the stairs to the balcony –*

A sound from the inconspicuous ottoman chest.

GRANDMA (*a whisper from the ottoman*). Youssef, I'm in here.

VICTOR *screams.*

(*From the ottoman.*) Victor? No fear, it's me!

YOUSSEF. Is that…?

GRANDMA (*from the ottoman*). Yoo-hoo.

YOUSSEF. God protect us!

GRANDMA (*from the ottoman*). Hello Youssef.

VICTOR. What the fuck!?

LOYS. Both of you please – he's tied up.

GRANDMA (*from the ottoman*). It's a mystery how she managed it… fear and love, fear and love – great motivators. When I was a boy, I saw my grandmother lift a tractor off her lover's face.

YOUSSEF (*whispers*). What happened?

LOYS (*whispers*).…sleeping pills in the stew…

GRANDMA (*from the ottoman*). Most clever. Now let's parlais – I think you'll find my terms agreeable.

VICTOR. Out the back now!

YOUSSEF. State them. Your terms.

VICTOR. What are you doing?

YOUSSEF. Just shut up a minute. State your terms.

GRANDMA. By right of the 1929 Geneva Treatise I insist on looking my captors in the eyes.

VICTOR. We have to run!

YOUSSEF. He'll find us.

VICTOR. How?!

YOUSSEF. He has eyes everywhere! Loys why didn't you run when you had the chance?!

LOYS. We can still run!

YOUSSEF. They'll burn the neighbourhood down.

GRANDMA (*from the ottoman*). This may come as a surprise but I actually don't go in for collective punishment. It's where the Old Testament and I part company. If you were to run, our retaliation would be specific. We'd start by burning Youssef and Faiza's house down. Then we'd round up your employees Victor. Loys, your choir and salon would be the final sugar on the bambolouni.

Beat.

YOUSSEF. Okay.

VICTOR. What are you doing?

YOUSSEF. We have to try and negotiate

LOYS. Don't – he'll talk us to death.

YOUSSEF *clears the rug and the coffee-table books off the ottoman chest.*

Opens the lid.

GRANDMA *sits up.*

GRANDMA. Hello mate.

YOUSSEF. State your terms.

GRANDMA. How's Mum?

LOYS. He knows your mum?

GRANDMA. Her rigatoni recipe is divine. And she instructed him so well. Loys, have you tried Youssef's rigatoni?

YOUSSEF. Tell us what you want.

GRANDMA. Victor, do you go in for rigatoni?

VICTOR….we should…

GRANDMA. Breathe Victor breathe.

VICTOR. Why are we talking to / him?

GRANDMA. Talking is the only way forward, and contrary to popular opinion there are only two directions of travel. Forwards and backwards.

VICTOR. There's an axe upstairs.

GRANDMA. Our retaliation on Tunisian Jewry will go beyond your darkest fears!

VICTOR *turns to go –*

Think! Before you sign a death warrant on your entire community. In the Ukraine, my men shot 33,771 Jews in two days. I tell you this not to provoke, rather to demonstrate our capacity.

LOYS. He has to disappear.

GRANDMA. If I disappear who will be blamed?

VICTOR. You don't scare us.

GRANDMA. Have you people learnt nothing from history!?

VICTOR. We're going to hurt you.

YOUSSEF. State your terms.

GRANDMA. Tell him to calm down!

YOUSSEF. Victor keep it together.

VICTOR. Keep it together we should be cutting him up!?

YOUSSEF. We're not like him habibi.

GRANDMA. I thought we were mates.

YOUSSEF. State your terms!

GRANDMA. What about the *sesh* we had last week?

LOYS. You drink with him?

YOUSSEF. When have I ever drunk!?

GRANDMA. Scout's honour Youssef only had orange juice.

YOUSSEF. Loys he's trying to turn / us against

GRANDMA. As a mixer!!

YOUSSEF. May you burn for this lie.

GRANDMA. Be honest Youssef, was the spirit of friendship
not present in our session last week – the way you
unburdened yourself – your inarticulacy – which I took as
you confessing feelings for the first time… about the woman,
the woman you were in love with –

VICTOR. Shut the top!

GRANDMA. Are you the cuckold?

YOUSSEF. He's lying Victor.

GRANDMA. I've been there Vic, we're kindred spirits

VICTOR. Someone shut him up!

GRANDMA. Only I killed the man who was pleasuring my wife!

LOYS. Victor you realise he's – he's trying to twist, I would never, Victor look at me, look at me –

VICTOR *shrugs* LOYS *off him, walks away.* YOUSSEF *follows him.*

YOUSSEF (*to* VICTOR). Habibi you must see he's trying to turn us against each other. You can't possibly believe – as if I could ever do something like that to you.

VICTOR *punches* YOUSSEF *in the face.*
YOUSSEF *falls into the fountain.*
Springs to his feet.
VICTOR *and* YOUSSEF *stay coiled, ready to pounce on each other.*

GRANDMA. I couldn't shake off my belief in monogamy either Vic – we're old-school. It's about fidelity, loyalty, but maybe you could be try and be more modern, renounce your monogamy, and you Loys on the brink of renouncing Zionism, how brave, your polyamory extends to *thought*, bravo! Bravo! –

YOUSSEF *picks up the knife and holds it to* GRANDMA's *throat.*

YOUSSEF. Your terms.

GRANDMA. Steady on my boy.

YOUSSEF. I'll do it.

GRANDMA. Clench this image in your mind for the future. It's the moment you became a politician.

LOYS. Cut his throat.

GRANDMA. In my pocket is a set of keys for a white Citroën, registration WTH 933. It is parked on Salambo Street. I want to pick up that car. Drive it off into the sunrise. Start over.

LOYS. The minute you leave you'll alert your men.

GRANDMA. Why would I want to?

VICTOR. Because you're a Nazi!

GRANDMA. Am I?

VICTOR. We can't trust anything / he says.

GRANDMA. Ever since El Alamein we've lost our footing. My nickname may save me, but I'm not taking any chances. Set me free. The last thing I would do is sound the alarm, I intend to slip away into the night.

VICTOR. How can we trust a murderer a rapist!?

GRANDMA. Who says I'm a rapist?

VICTOR. What did you come to this house for?!

GRANDMA. Inform your husband there was no hanky-panky.

VICTOR. Cos she drugged you!

GRANDMA. Loys knows, women know when a man's intention is *rapey*.

LOYS. I have no idea what is going through your head.

GRANDMA. On the accusation of rape – I will speak the truth. Last night my intention was only sups and chats. I'll admit, as the evening progressed the wine and intellectual back-and-forth started to stimulate me in all sorts of regions, regions that have been foreign to me for a very long time. Usually I have no compulsion but last night Loys, you bewitched me. I felt a fire in my groin, my heart panting, conscience gone for dust, hold on it's a happy ending folks because somehow, somewhere I managed to cling on to some residue of humanity, I freed myself from the blinding white heat of desire – shut up and fell asleep.

VICTOR. Why are we listening to this?!

LOYS. Maybe we should burn him.

VICTOR. They'll see the smoke. We chop him up, scatter him on the hillside.

YOUSSEF *reaches into* GRANDMA*'s pockets and takes out the keys.*

YOUSSEF. Both of you shut up, who wants to go?

VICTOR. You're not thinking of setting him free!?

YOUSSEF. We need a car!

LOYS. It's a trap. Salambo Street, there's a Nazi depot on Salambo Street.

GRANDMA. You think German soldiers will be working at this time?

YOUSSEF. I'll go.

LOYS. *Youssef* – a Nazi depot – in the middle of the night!?

YOUSSEF. I'm going.

GRANDMA. Better Victor goes, you're hurt.

VICTOR *walks upstairs*.

YOUSSEF. Victor?

VICTOR. I'm going to find that axe.

YOUSSEF. Victor come back.

LOYS. Check the roof, in the shed.

YOUSSEF. Loys?

VICTOR. It used to hang in the study.

LOYS. I did a clear-out.

VICTOR. Oh, okay. (*From the upstairs balcony.*) Always did look odd in the study.

VICTOR *disappears*.

LOYS *and* YOUSSEF *forget* GRANDMA *for a second and look at each other.*

GRANDMA. And god created man and woman in his image, to be fruitful and multiply, to conquer the earth.

LOYS. We should cut out your tongue.

GRANDMA. Ble gll ooo mmm aaa glluuuuuuh rrrrr – is my impression of man with no tongue. Let me translate what he just said. I can arrange safe passage for the two of you.

A new start where your love can grow unimpeded. Where would you like to go – New York? Buenos Aires? Santiago Chile?

LOYS *tries to close the lid but* GRANDMA *bites at her.*

Practise what you preach Loys, build a life with a lover from outside your tribe.

LOYS. Shut the lid.

GRANDMA. Why should Victor or Faiza stand in your way?

LOYS. Youseff!

GRANDMA. Why die as a monogamous Zionist?! The man you love is right in front of you – grab him close – never let him go – live true – what is the point of living if you don't try and live true!?

LOYS *picks up the knife and runs at* GRANDMA*, who ducks –* LOYS *shuts the lid.*

LOYS. You should have shut the lid.

YOUSSEF. Are you going to dismiss it all?

LOYS. The ravings of a desperate man?

YOUSSEF. I'd like to live true.

LOYS. There are many truths – the man talks like a virgin.

YOUSSEF. Seeing Victor, perhaps it stirred something.

LOYS. Stop –

YOUSSEF. Have your feelings changed?

Beat.

LOYS. Faiza is carrying life.

YOUSSEF. I'll leave her.

LOYS. You won't, you can't.

YOUSSEF. I will.

LOYS. You didn't even have the courage to tell me, how could you ever leave –

YOUSSEF. I'm ready.

LOYS. You'd shame Faiza like that?

YOUSSEF. She'd remarry.

LOYS. If you die – not if you walk out on her!

YOUSSEF. Where can we go?

LOYS. I should go with someone who leaves their wife and child?!

YOUSSEF. I'd never do that to you.

LOYS. How can I trust you?

YOUSSEF. You must. Where should we go?

LOYS. Your heart isn't free.

YOUSSEF. It could be! Why must we return to our marriages?

LOYS. I quite like my marriage, you quite like yours.

YOUSSEF. (No this is more!) Last night, as we rode into the darkness – someone started firing – in that moment… I thought of you – only of you – *Your face*. In the camp I stayed sane imagining *you*. Our future somewhere, living together, sitting in our own courtyard, you drinking Boukha and smoking, me sipping mint tea with a shisha, cards, books, children –

LOYS. That story – that clarity! I don't believe / it.

YOUSSEF. After what we've tasted!?

LOYS. What have we *tasted*!? Forbidden fruit!?

YOUSSEF. We're much much / more than

LOYS. And we're mistaking that taste for something else.

YOUSSEF. Come on Loys, be brave

LOYS. You were my plaything,

YOUSSEF. That's not true.

LOYS. We were each other's playthings.

YOUSSEF. A quick fuck?

LOYS. ...a time and a place.

YOUSSEF. We talked and loved talked and loved.

LOYS. We were scared, we escaped, the drama of it all –

YOUSSEF. At the beginning yes... but then something shifted... didn't it?

Beat.

LOYS *holds* YOUSSEF.

LOYS. How can we run away together. You told a Nazi where I live.

YOUSSEF. Loys...

VICTOR *appears on the balcony carrying a large pitchfork.*

VICTOR. Did you throw out the axe?

LOYS. It's in the shed, near the gardening tools.

VICTOR. Trust me, it's not there.

LOYS. You obviously didn't look properly.

VICTOR. I went through the whole fucking shed.

LOYS. Is that blood?

VICTOR. Paint. I used it when I dressed up as a scarecrow for Purim.

YOUSSEF. Put the pitchfork down Victor.

VICTOR. It'll do the job, chopping him up might be / tricky

YOUSSEF. Okay I'm going.

LOYS. You're leaving us surrounded by Nazis!

YOUSSEF. They'd never dare interrupt Grandma.

VICTOR. We should castrate him.

YOUSSEF. I'll get the car. We'll drive over the border, hand him to the Americans...

LOYS. What about Faiza?

Beat.

YOUSSEF. We'll pick up Faiza on the way out of the city.

Beat.

LOYS. You're hurt – I'll go.

YOUSSEF. I'm fine.

GRANDMA *opens the lid of the chest with his head.*

GRANDMA. Youssef you're wounded. What would be quickest is if *I go* and then drive back here and pick you up.

VICTOR. That's not / happening.

GRANDMA. Then you should go Victor – wear my uniform –

LOYS. Youssef wait –

YOUSSEF. I'll be back in the hour.

GRANDMA. You won't make it back before sunrise, send someone healthy! Send Loys – nobody will bother Loys – don't leave – Youssef – my Arabian brother – remember the conversations – the dreams – the dreams –

YOUSSEF *spits in* GRANDMA*'s face.*

YOUSSEF *walks to the upstairs balcony.*

YOUSSEF. Keep Victor on a leash.

VICTOR. May your wound lead to sepsis

LOYS....

YOUSSEF....

YOUSSEF *exits.*

GRANDMA. Would you be so kind to wipe that spittle off?

Beat.

VICTOR *and* LOYS *stare at* GRANDMA.

Might you excuse me? This old biddy needs a nap.

GRANDMA *ceremoniously leans back into the ottoman.*

Be a dear and close the lid.

VICTOR *closes the lid.*

GRANDMA *sings 'White Christmas', stopping after '...merry and bright'.*

LOYS. You need to eat.

LOYS *exits to the kitchen.*

VICTOR *pours himself a glass of Boukha.*

LOYS *re-enters with kemia – on the plate are olives, an egg, tuna, a dish with harissa sauce, pickled carrots, cauliflower florets, turnips.*

VICTOR *eats like an animal.*

Stops eating. Looks at LOYS, *ashamed.*

It's okay, eat how you / like.

VICTOR. No, I'm at home now.

VICTOR *forces himself to eat slowly.*

LOYS *lights a cigarette.*

LOYS. Do you mind if I smoke?

VICTOR. Of course not.

Beat.

Join me with a Boukha?

LOYS. Later.

Beat.

Did you make any new friends in the camp?

VICTOR. Eh?

LOYS. Sorry, is that a stupid question?

VICTOR. No, it's... Youssef was obviously around.

LOYS. Who else? Who else did you talk to?

VICTOR. There was always someone.

LOYS. Not much privacy?

VICTOR....more of a communal... experience.

LOYS....

At the beginning I'd lie awake trying to picture you. I imagined you chatting with other men, like you'd all gone... camping. (How foolish.)

VICTOR....you'd be surprised...

LOYS. Tell me.

VICTOR. Some evenings were like that. In their own way.

LOYS. That's, that's good.

VICTOR *has finished eating.*

He lights a cigarette. Stares at LOYS.

VICTOR. I made a friend called Maurice.

LOYS. What's Maurice like?

VICTOR. Bit of a prankster.

LOYS. I'm sure you got on famously.

VICTOR. In some ways we're quite different... he's a tailor.

A few weeks ago Maurice cut his leg. He wrapped it in a bandage, but during work, the bandage kept slipping down. Every time Maurice bent down to pull it up, he'd make a little sound, like a trombone. *Bwaah*. We often worked side by side so the whole day I'd be hearing this *Bwaah*, and it never stopped being funny, the Nazis, the guards, everyone found it hilarious. Then one afternoon the clouds were dark and someone predicted it was going to snow. An officer ordered a hole to be dug. After work, Maurice was sent to sleep outside in the hole. It didn't snow that night but the temperatures dropped. The next morning, Maurice was a block of ice. I sat with a cup and waited for him to thaw. Whatever melted off him... I could drink.
Has that story swayed you?

LOYS. Huh?

VICTOR. I've shown you loyalty, concern, friendship but heat, we're nothing without heat.

Beat.

LOYS. The occupation has made us not ourselves.

VICTOR. What if it has revealed us? I've done things.

LOYS. You were a prisoner.

VICTOR. A prisoner has choices. He can share his bread. Or he can hoard it.

LOYS. That guilt. Pay it no attention.

VICTOR. Is that how you get by?

Beat.

LOYS. Ask me what you need to ask me. If you think it will help.

Beat.

VICTOR. In the land of milk and honey... in the land of milk and honey... we'll tell each other everything.

It's coming up to the hour.

LOYS. Perhaps he's gone to the hospital.

VICTOR. Perhaps.
Or.
He's skipped town with Faiza. Maybe he's at a brothel. Or the mosque. That's the thing about Youssef, there's more than meets the eye.
You think you know someone and then they dazzle you.

LOYS. He risked his life saving you.

VICTOR. Have you ever seen a Nazi hurt an Arab? They're too busy noshing them off, hoping to take this occupation to the next stage.
Am I too coarse?

LOYS. I didn't say that.

VICTOR. You winced.

LOYS. Please let's not fight.

VICTOR. I've never had the grace of Youssef.

LOYS. Victor –

VICTOR. I was always too loud, and my language – you didn't like the words I chose, too certain, you always said, as if being certain is a bad thing – you're ashamed of me you're so ashamed but you never had the courage to say it. How pathetic, lusting after some penniless dreamer, whose gentleness you misread for some sort of of of integrity but where is he, where is he?!

LOYS. Victor… I have made mistakes… I'm willing to –

VICTOR. Are you surprised he's left?

LOYS. Can we stop talking about Youssef.

VICTOR. Is it a shock him abandoning you?

LOYS. You have to move on, if we have any hope of a future.

VICTOR. Is your heart breaking?

LOYS. Shut up!

VICTOR. Your heart breaking for a dog, a dog with the soul of a rat, a horror that should have died in the womb – there'll be no paradise for that Arab, justice will be an eternity in a hole, starving, bleeding, foaming at the mouth...

LOYS. So I fucked him! Now you're back. Let's get on with our lives.

Pause.

VICTOR. If it was just a fuck why haven't we left?

LOYS. We need a car.

VICTOR. That's an excuse, you want him, you still want him.

LOYS. I don't.

VICTOR. You do.

LOYS. I could have left months ago – *I waited for you.*

VICTOR. I think you change your mind ever single second.

LOYS. It's clear now.

VICTOR. I don't know who you are... I need to go... I need to go...

LOYS. Tell me how I can prove it!?

VICTOR. When your husband suggests a road trip – don't invite your lover and his Nazi mate!

LOYS. Okay.

LOYS *picks up the knife. Opens the lid.*

GRANDMA *sits up, startled.*

VICTOR. Loys what are you doing – put the knife –

LOYS. It's the only way.

VICTOR. You don't need to do this – we can run, let's just run

GRANDMA. Youssef will never see past it.

LOYS. I know.

GRANDMA. Why settle for sorbet?!

LOYS *calmly sticks the knife into* GRANDMA*'s heart.*

Cunt.

LOYS *withdraws the knife. Plunges it into* GRANDMA*'s neck.*

VICTOR *starts stabbing* GRANDMA *with the pitchfork.*

GRANDMA *is dead.*

VICTOR. Did he touch you?

LOYS. (What?) No.

VICTOR. He would've, if you hadn't've drugged him.

LOYS. Perhaps.

VICTOR. Certainly a murderer... seen that with my own eyes...

LOYS. How could Youssef have told him our address?

Beat.

VICTOR. It's okay, it's over now, we don't have to worry about any of that now.

LOYS. (It was you.) Uh

LOYS *is trembling, she turns away from* VICTOR.

A key opens the front door. YOUSSEF *walks in.* LOYS *and* VICTOR *stare at him.*

VICTOR. (You came back.)

YOUSSEF. The street's empty. They must have driven back to camp. I've got the car. It's parked on the other side of the hill. We should still leave out the back. Just in case. It'll be quicker if Grandma walks with us, rather than carrying him, when we get to the car we can put him in the boot, maybe give him some water and food first so he doesn't – (*Notices* GRANDMA.) god have mercy.

(Victor) what have you done?

VICTOR. Are you going to cry?

YOUSSEF. We'll all be shot, our families will be shot.

VICTOR. Nobody needs to get shot! We get him out of the house, the plan stays –

YOUSSEF. What – what plan?

VICTOR. Drive out of the city, dump him in the / countryside

YOUSSEF. Why Victor?

LOYS. I did it.

YOUSSEF....

VICTOR. I helped.

YOUSSEF. That isn't, that's not, that that can't *be*.

LOYS. That's how it is.

YOUSSEF. Did he attack you?

LOYS. No.

YOUSSEF....

The adhan starts to sound out over the city.

VICTOR (*to* YOUSSEF). Take his head, I'll take his legs.

YOUSSEF. Leave Grandma here.

VICTOR. What?

YOUSSEF. Leave him here.

LOYS. If they find him they'll do exactly what we fear they'll do.

YOUSSEF. I'll make him disappear before it comes to that.

Beat.

VICTOR. Come on Loys, it's getting light.

LOYS. It's Passover in a few hours. Thousands of houses will be burning their bread. Tunis will be full of smoke.

YOUSSEF *douses the chest in Boukha.*
All three pick up the candles circling the courtyard and drop them in the chest.

The flames start to lick.

We can still pick up Faiza and go.

Beat.

YOUSSEF. I don't think she'd want to leave.

The sun starts to rise.

VICTOR. Shall we?

LOYS. ... Yes.

YOUSSEF *hands the car keys to* VICTOR.

VICTOR *slowly turns away from* LOYS *and* YOUSSEF.

LOYS *and* YOUSSEF *look at each other.*

LOYS *grabs her bag and* VICTOR, *they walk up the stairs to the balcony and disappear.*

YOUSSEF *looks at the fire.*

The lights fade.

A polite knock at the door.

YOUSSEF *moves to run up the stairs.*
Turns around.
Sits.

THUMP THUMP THUMP AT THE DOOR.

YOUSSEF. Just looking for my keys!

YOUSSEF *remains sat.*

Boots start to kick at the door.

Hold on – just putting out the fire – we don't want smoke going in your eyes – you should have got here earlier, I made chicken couscous. I can't recommend it enough. You'll need plenty of harissa, garlic, olive oil. Throw in some carrots and courgettes. Chickpeas! Soaked overnight. And then serve with a plate of olives. Always get your olives from Djerba – they're the best in the world. The couscous, make sure it's fluffy and moist –

GUNSHOTS from outside the door, trying to shoot the lock open.

Little Fella! Memento! There's something in the fire! Praise be to god she's here – Kahina is here! Kahina in La Marsa. Oh my god her hair! It's streaming out over the entire courtyard. How blessed you are! To meet our prophet on the battlefield! And don't be fooled, she may look a hundred and twenty-seven but Kahina has two lovers. There's a woman in town who can summon her… she was here earlier, I just missed her… praise be Kahina stuck around… shush… quiet! Kahina is talking. (*He listens to the fire.*) 'The Blonds are faulty.' (*He listens.*) 'They can only lecture or rape' – Kahina likes a man that can listen and love – (*He listens.*)

...oh. Oh dear. I've got some news boys.
You're about to die. Now don't be sad. There are worse
places to die.
Look at La Marsa in the afternoon,
all the white sheets strung up on washing lines,
floating in the sun.

YOUSSEF *takes in a big breath.*

The End.

www.nickhernbooks.co.uk

facebook.com/nickhernbooks

twitter.com/nickhernbooks